The Power of Negative Thinking

INTRODUCTION

Many of us are not aware of our optimistic tendencies. . . . Data clearly shows that most people overestimate their prospects for professional achievement; expect their children to be extraordinarily gifted; miscalculate their likely life span; expect to be healthier than their peers; hugely underestimate their likelihood of divorce, cancer, and unemployment; and are confident overall that their future lives will be better than those their parents put up with. This is known as the optimism bias — the inclination to overestimate the likelihood of encountering positive events in the future and to underestimate the likelihood of experiencing negative events.

> — *The Optimism Bias: A Tour of the*
> *Irrationally Positive Brain*
> (TALI SHAROT, PANTHEON BOOKS, 2011)

THERE IS, ADMITTEDLY, a large helping of my version of humor in the title chosen for this book, an obvious play on a work that has been almost a bible for much of America most of my lifetime: *The Power of Positive Thinking* by Norman Vincent Peale.

It came out in 1952, when I was in elementary school. It

sold more than two million copies its first year out, and it's still in print, with total copies sold now over five million. Taking the opposite position starts me out millions of books behind in the sales race. I'm very comfortable being a contrarian and stating my argument for *The Power of Negative Thinking*.

I didn't know, until I did a little research for this book, that Norman Vincent Peale also is from northern Ohio. We're separated by two generations, born and reared about 100 miles apart; he's from the western side of the state, and I hail from the east. That makes us products of pretty much the same middle-American, small-town upbringing and culture, each of us even raised in the same Methodist denomination. He switched to Dutch Reformed; I am more of a theological free agent, though definitely more theo- than atheo-.

For all his book-selling, preaching, lecturing, and TV success, the Rev. Mr. Peale did have his disbelievers. His partner in a couple of earlier psychological-theological books split with him over *The Power of Positive Thinking*. Thought it could be dangerous. To at least some degree, so does Tali Sharot, apparently.

There is a story that Democratic presidential candidate Adlai Stevenson was advised before a campaign speaking appearance at a church that he probably wouldn't get any votes out of the audience, because Bishop Peale had urged his followers to vote as a bloc for Republican candidate Dwight D. Eisenhower. His own biblical knowledge — and wit — showing, Stevenson quipped in response: "I find Paul appealing and Peale appalling."

I was too young to vote at the time, but I'm sure I'd have gone for Eisenhower over Stevenson both times they ran. Still, give Stevenson his due — he knew what it meant to be an underdog and kept his sense of humor.

Beneath the irony of turning Peale upside down, her book offers a thesis that I have advocated for years. Ms. Sharot is described on her book jacket as a researcher "on optimism, memory, and emotion" with "a Ph.D. in psychology and neuroscience from New York University," and a research fellow at the Wellcome Trust, among other academic positions. In Orrville, Ohio, that would raise skeptical eyebrows, but it is interesting company for a basketball coach.

In her book *The Optimism Bias,* Ms. Sharot states:

> The reality is that most people perceive themselves as being superior to the average human being. . . . A survey conducted in the mid-1970s revealed that 85 percent ranked themselves in the top 50th percentile for the ability to get along well with others and 70 percent did so for leadership ability. . . . Another survey showed that 91 percent believed they were in the top 50th percentile for driving ability. . . . [I]mpossible. Most people cannot be better than most people. . . . We can, however, all believe that we are at the high end on most positive attributes, and indeed we do. This is known as the superiority illusion.

I don't agree totally with her conclusions. I'm a basketball coach who tends from experience and instinct to see more graphically the things she describes intellectually. But I whole-heartedly agree that we as people and as a nation are by nature inclined to see things optimistically—above and beyond any push in that direction by the Rev. Mr. Peale. And I do see some dangers in that—as I did for more than forty years of coaching college basketball. What seems too good to be true usually is—there is a genuine need to be cautious, to look both ways before crossing any streets in life. Paying attention to the downside is a difficult but essential quality for achieving long-term success in any occupation or family situation.

Throughout this book, I will speak largely as a coach, in coaching and basketball terms. And since my turf was men's basketball, I am going to be using the "he" pronoun more than "she." But I intend everything to be interpreted much more broadly than that, for both sexes and metaphorically, because the principles I established and followed in coaching carry over perfectly to the way I think leadership works best in business or any other area of life. Coaching is leadership, and leadership is leadership, whether in a gym, an office, a classroom, or a family.

Let me be clear: I am *not* arguing for being a strict negativist, for walking around with a sour look, for always seeing the dark side, always expecting failure. That's not my intent at all. Quite the opposite.

I'm saying that being alert to the possible negatives in any situation is the very best way to bring about positive results. And the reverse is true, too—ignoring or failing to spot potential hazards in advance makes failure all the more likely. For example, I'm talking about being aware that it *can* rain. You can plan the greatest outdoor event in the world—food, games, entertainment, decorations—but if a rain shower would turn everything into chaos and you don't allow for that possibility, you're risking disaster because of blind optimism.

Don't be caught thinking something is going to work just because you *think* it's going to work.

Planning beats repairing.

And good planning avoids the need for fixing up a project that plowed ahead without thought at all about potential pitfalls.

Stop and think. That's a phrase we've all used to introduce a new way of considering something, to argue for stepping back from a situation and looking at it in an all-new light.

Stop and think: That's what I'm saying is always the best approach before rushing forward with carried-away zeal.

One of our most lauded qualities is the ability to think fast. In an emergency, that's great. But it's also risky. When time permits, it's much better to be sure you're thinking clearly. How many times have we read or heard of someone who made a rash decision and now faces criminal charges, or lost his job, or broke his family apart by an unwise act? There are so many unintended consequences in any important action that we need to at least consider, like the best chess player, how our next move could produce an unexpected chain reaction down the line.

I'm expressing the case for making *sure,* for *not* taking success for granted . . . for *getting* that regular mammogram or rectal exam . . . for protecting health and life and possessions with insurance . . . for planning your retirement in the prime income years; in short, for the wisdom and value represented by the simple, common sense of *The Power of Negative Thinking.*

I want you to feel provoked by this book, perhaps to learn from it, and certainly to have some fun and be entertained as we change your prescription on your rose-colored glasses.

COACH BOB KNIGHT

The Power of Negative Thinking

Keep Pollyanna on the Bench

DON'T WORRY, HONEY. Everything will be all-l-l right."

Chances are the first time you heard that was from your mother when you were three or four years old. It's dangerous and borderline un-American to speak out against any form of motherly advice, but let's be honest about this one:

"Let me kiss it and make it well."

The truth is that unless Mom had a mouthful of iodine, she probably wasn't going to help. Whatever led to that soothing assurance was not going to turn out all right until medication — not mollification — was used.

From infancy up we're inundated with platitudes that may provide short-term diversion but don't work in the long run.

No, time does *not* heal all wounds. Not by itself. Time *can,* if it is used to recognize what caused the wounds, do something to eliminate the cause of the distress. Better yet, we can try to prevent it. To negate it.

Hence: *The Power of Negative Thinking.*

The power we all have to let Pollyanna exist only in fairy tales will make our own life work much better by eliminating the false illusions that create or compound our problems by pretending they don't exist.

I think there *is* a lot of Pollyanna — characterized by irrepressible optimism and a tendency to find good in everything — in the book title that made Norman Vincent Peale a lot of money and eternally famous. The Power of Pollyanna Thinking, if practiced indiscriminately, can be reckless and dangerous. Why don't we want Pollyanna on our team? I speak as a coach whose career-long belief was that *most* basketball games are *not won,* they are *lost.* I always looked at upcoming games and saw all kinds of ways we could lose to our next opponent, some of them — maybe most of them — things that had nothing to do with the opponent at all but involved what we had to correct about our own execution to keep from beating ourselves.

Think of a game strategy the way a great sculptor looks at a slab of marble. He or she wants to scrape away the unnecessary bulk until the proper contours of the figures emerge.

Negative material is eliminated to create a harmonious work of art.

As I looked ahead to every game and every season, my first thought was always: *What vulnerabilities do we have and what can we do to minimize them, to get around them, to survive them — and give ourselves a better chance to win?* In effect, how do you eliminate the wasted energy and unnecessary mistakes to build a cohesive and successful team that can play within its strengths?

I put up signs in the locker room making clear things I wanted to stress, certain basic principles that I wanted each player on my team to see every day from the start of practice through the last game of the year. These would become etched so firmly and clearly in the players' minds that they would become second nature.

The one I always posted first because I thought it was the most important said: *Victory favors the team making the fewest mistakes.* Every team I coached dressed for practice or games under a sign that said that. Another of my favorites; When the Burger King advertising slogan was "Have it your way," I told our players: "This ain't Burger King. We'll do it *my* way."

Basketball — like life — *is* at least partly a game of mistakes. Despite thousands of years of evolutionary improvements, human beings do not play any game perfectly. As a coach, you have to understand, it's not the development of your offense or the development of your defense that will make you a consistently winning team; it's the elimination of mistakes — it's getting rid of those things that amount to a deal-breaker in the game of basketball:

Poor ball handling

Bad shots

Slow recovery from offense to defense

Bad fouls and poor foul-shooting

Poor blocking out of opponents in rebounding

Go-it-alone, uncoordinated defense

These are *individual* mistakes or lazy instances of irresponsible carelessness that cause *teams* to fail. Think in business terms: In success, a hotdogging and credit-grabbing CEO or department head hogs the glory — and in failure blames others. Of course, that leader's colleagues boil with resentment, which at some point turns to sloppiness. In sports jargon, they take their eye off the ball, off the focus of what the company needs from them. As a coach or a leader, you are responsible for bringing out the best from your "team," not causing the worst.

Before you can inspire your players to "win," you have to show them how not to lose. In basketball, bad fouls top my list of bad habits. A bad foul comes from poor concentration by a player responsible for carrying out a defensive assignment—a grab, a hold, a play that violates every fundamental we spend hours teaching on the practice floor about footwork, proper defensive stance, alertness, anticipation. It's a foul that just should not have been committed, a shortcut—like many shortcuts around established procedures and rules—that just should not have been taken. In basketball, it can give an opponent two free points and add to the team-foul count, too. As a business practice, this is a failure to hold up a personal responsibility that jeopardizes a whole team effort.

Elimination of this kind of team letdown is why I always treated the practice floor like a classroom, demanding full attention and concentration. I wanted the basketball classroom to be more demanding than any course in the whole university.

Out there on the court, not only were there principles to be learned, there wasn't immediate practical application of those theories. These exercises were not designed to be fun. Sometimes coaches talk about the "fun" in practice and "fun" in preparing for a game. I've never felt there was "fun" in either one. The fun comes with winning. One of my favorite players ever, Mike Gyovai, who defined toughness playing for us as a six-foot-five center at Army, touched on that subject when he made a few remarks at a West Point dinner. "I can tell you that, as a class, we did not have *fun* playing basketball—

as a matter of fact, I did not have fun here, when you get right down to it," he said. "I didn't come here to have fun. I came here to play basketball and win games, and become a solider, and that's what we did." He learned how to win.

The act of winning, the art of winning, and knowing how to win were critical attributes for a future officer. And, winning is the goal, the defining mark of success, in almost any job — even the clergy, I'm guessing.

The If-Don't Syndrome

So many negative things can be done in the game of basketball that you have to address them, in terms of those four words that are at the heart of this negative-to-achieve positive manifesto: We have no chance to win *if* . . . We're going to get our ass beat *unless* . . . We *can't* play this way . . . This is something that you *don't* do . . . and win. The most sickening feelings for a loser are "woulda-coulda-shoulda." Prepare your team to prepare and execute properly, to curtail its mistakes, and the most painful aftermaths of losing will be minimized — but never avoided.

Watching game film with my team was a great way to attack mistakes. Some coaches like to use those sessions to call out good plays. I wanted to pinpoint mistakes — and especially patterns of mistakes — so they wouldn't occur again. We won

a lot of games, a lot of championships, over the years by pol-
ishing the things that our own team did well, but in our preparations always focusing, above all, on preventing losing. That
included locking in on what the other team did well, what the
other team could do to beat us — when they had the ball, when
we had the ball, or when the ball was up for grabs on the floor
and possession was available to either team.

Everyone Has Desire

My list of hollow platitudes includes the idea that You Can Do
Anything You Really Want to Do. The truth is you can't. Chalk
it up to the Divine Being's grand plan for making the whole
world work because of interdependence, but the fact is each of
us has more things that we cannot do well than we can. That's
why society has doctors and plumbers and electricians and
mechanics and every other Craigslist specialist.

Nobody worked harder than I did in trying to motivate
and inspire our players to play with passion, and in trying to
keep a team's focus on doing all the "little" things that are really huge things — hustle and desire and heart and will and determination. If you play with passion, you are also more likely
to play with precision, because the more your players have in-
vested in effort and energy in trying to win a game, the more
effort and energy come out in a game. But I wince every time

I hear an announcer say in the last seconds of a close game, "Now we'll see which team *wants* it the most."

Somebody will win, somebody will lose, but don't ever tell me the difference every time is that the winner wanted to win more than the loser did.

Let me give a recent example: Duke versus Butler for the 2010 NCAA men's basketball championship. Just about everybody in America was lined up behind Butler, splendidly coached by young Brad Stevens and a national Cinderella darling for coming from one of the smaller leagues and pushing aside the big-name teams all along the way to reach the championship game. They tell me everybody hates Duke, because they win so much. I love Duke, because they win so much — because, under a coach I think a lot of, Mike Krzyzewski, they play the game a little bit better a little more often than all those teams they're beating. That night I had great admiration for both teams, because I was really impressed with what Brad Stevens and his kids had done.

So I just sat back and watched two teams play very hard and go at each other with well-planned and well-executed defenses. And when a couple of last-minute Butler shots — one makeable and one a Hail Mary from half-court that did come close — missed, Duke won and Butler didn't.

Now, some guy on TV is going to try to tell me that the

game came out as it did because Duke *wanted* it more? I'm one of those TV guys now but I try not to say dumb things like that. Nobody could have *wanted* to win that game more than those Butler kids . . . *or* those Duke kids.

Wanting alone doesn't get anything done.

Doing does. Duke that night *did* just a little bit more. Or, in my terms, they made fewer mistakes and played within their disciplined training to take home the championship.

Afterward, when Brad Stevens and his Butler coaching staff sat down and went over the tape of that game — not the easiest thing to do after a big disappointment but a critical part of the coaching education — I'll bet those missed shots at the end weren't even among those coaches' reasons for Butler's loss.

My definition of discipline, particularly in basketball but much more widely applicable than that, comes into play here:

> *Discipline is recognizing what has to be done, doing it as well as you can do it, and doing it that way all the time.*

Of course you won't do your best every time. Discipline involves *trying* to do your best every time.

The difference between knowing what you should do and repeatedly trying to do it is the same as is pointed out in another maxim of mine:

Having the will to win is not enough. Everyone has that. What matters is having the will to prepare to win.

That will to prepare addresses what I'm focusing on here.

The Power of Negative Thinking comes into play by recognizing, addressing, and removing the obstacles to winning.

Losing Is for . . . Losers

I have seen all kinds of books about winning, often by athletes or business executives whose lifelong record of victories (or profits) is dubious.

I haven't seen one intelligent book yet about losing.

There should be one, because every coach — every person — has to deal with losing. The first essential to have in place — in your mind, at least — is a plan to recover after a loss, to *learn* from a loss, to eliminate those things that caused a loss.

Learning from a loss doesn't make it a good loss. Late in our 1975–76 season at Indiana, I'm absolutely sure that Al McGuire, whose Marquette team was No. 2 in the country at the time, was being honest, and not trying to play head games with our team, when he said it would be best for us, as far as winning the national championship was concerned, to lose a regular-season game, to take off the "pressure" of a long winning streak. I didn't agree with Al, then or now — 37 years later.

And I'm sure the players on that 1975–76 Indiana team are

as proud as their coach that we were the last major college men's team that never got the "pressure" off. Every champion since has lost at least *two* games.

But I always felt that when you did lose, it was imperative that you learn from the loss. *Why* did we lose? If we lost simply because they had better players, we'd need to recruit better players. But the vast majority of time, it's going to go back to mistakes. That's where constant focus has to be.

Coaches often inwardly if not publicly blame a loss on a bad call, an injury, or something unusual that happened in the game, when the real reason was mistakes. A typical press-conference comment from a losing coach is "They just shot lights-out," when the real reason "they" did was his defense allowed them to get good shots. Or "We couldn't hit a thing; our shooting was really off tonight," when the truth was "we" took too many bad shots, "we" did not work to get good shots — any team is always likely to miss *bad* shots.

Every team must play with confidence, but losing is a potential reality you'd better be thinking about — in a season, or in a game, any game, just as a banker or broker had better be thinking about downside risk in any investment.

And let me be clear: Preparing not to lose is designed to aid and abet winning. The object here is to win. It's not a character fault to detest losing.

You constantly hear that losing is part of sport that you

have to learn to accept. I made a conscious effort after losses to acknowledge what the other coach or team, or a specific player, had done especially well, but it probably isn't surprising that I don't buy the inevitability of losing—ever! I never wanted to be—or to depend on—a person who isn't bothered by losing. To me a good loser is probably someone who has had too much practice at it.

We Won, Great, Now Move On . . .

The positive thinker tends to enjoy a big win, to congratulate himself and his staff and his players and generally revel in the fact that he and his team won! The negative thinker has already forgotten that one and gone to work on the next game.

It happens so often it's predictable: A team plays well and pulls off what is considered to be a great upset, then gives away what it had gained by losing the next game, often to an inferior opponent.

I felt so strongly about that very situation that I had a name for the way I approached it: the Last Game–Next Game theory. In basketball, if I thought we had an insurmountable lead toward the end of a game where we had beaten a pretty good team, I'd pull our five starters and—while that game was still being played out and those starters were on the bench—I'd be talking to those five about the next game: getting them thinking about who they were going to guard, about what we were going to be facing, getting them over this game. I didn't want them gloating about how well we played in a game that was almost over.

That was not to deny them the satisfaction they deserved after a job well done. A coach should never forget to compliment his players on a well-played victory, but shouldn't hesitate to tell them when they've played poorly — in a loss or a win.

The mark of success, or failure, in handling victory is what happens the next time out. The best teams can always get from the last game to the next game and be ready to play. My experience is that the positive thinker has a real tendency to savor the fruits of victory, to stay with this great win, so of course his *team* does the same thing.

Here is a primary place where negative thinking — realizing how that happy moment can beat you the next time out — makes a big difference between winning and losing. Get on to the next game. Enjoy those "big" wins when the season is over.

Think back on them then and smile all you want, but not when that "big" win of yours has already given whoever you're playing in your next game all the more desire to beat you and profit from your achievement. I always tried to emphasize that with my teams: "Don't let this team coming up take away what you earned the last game." The greatest victory is eliminated by lack of follow-up.

One game is not a season. Pleasure, enjoyment, success are not short-term. Success is a grind. It's perseverance; it is operating at a high level of performance on a constant basis.

That victory smile followed by a loser's stumble can happen in business, too. The good don't let up and neither do the great. Jim Collins, the business guru, has observed that "good is the enemy of great" because if we're too easily satisfied, we lose our edge.

Suffering in Defeat

Retired baseball manager Tony La Russa is one of those absolute greats who never loses that edge. For a long time now, dating back to his Oakland days, I've considered Tony a close and good friend. And I've admired the hell out of him, for the way he approaches his job, and does it — his ability to be objectively critical of his players and himself.

I was elated when he managed the St. Louis Cardinals to the 2011 World Series championship — and at least as elated, maybe more so, when a few days after that he announced his retirement. He was going out at the very pinnacle, the top. Another great manager and close La Russa friend, Jim Leyland of the Detroit Tigers, said a case can be made that Tony was the all-time best manager in baseball history. And I think he's right. Tony's teams won more games than any manager in the last sixty years, and he won three World Series. Focus on that alone. How many other guys won three World Series championships without the benefit of overwhelming budgets and rosters full of high-priced stars?

His critics said he over-managed. I think he over-won.

I've sat in the dugout with Tony at spring training games. He has sat on my bench during games, during practices, during team meetings. I've had dinner with him a hundred times. I've talked baseball, made out batting orders, discussed strategy, even unorthodox ideas such as hitting the pitcher eighth in the order (rather than ninth) in order to put more get-on-base guys immediately in front of sluggers like Albert Pujols and Mark McGwire.

I've studied Tony after wins and after losses. A friend of mine saw him at those two extremes, too, and said he didn't think there was another soul on earth who hit the depths after a loss that I do—until he saw Tony and thought: "This guy plays 162 games a year and suffers like that!" I loved him for that kind of passion, that much caring.

And then I read some things he said the day he retired:

Coaches tell me all the time, "You don't enjoy the wins like you suffer the losses," and there's a lot of truth to that. You lose, the next day you can't put it away, you win and it's usually easy because you're worried about the next one.

Tony had gone through one of the most difficult challenges along that line in his next-to-last game: Game 6 of that great 2011 World Series, when the Texas Rangers had St. Louis down 3 games to 2, and led late in the game that would have clinched the Series for them. The Cardinals were down 7–5 with two outs and two strikes in the 9th, then 9–7 with two outs and two strikes in the 10th, before St. Louis won on a home run in the bottom of the 11th. Twice they had come back to tie the score against almost overwhelming odds and then won with a walk-off home run an inning later.

Now the series was tied at three games apiece, and after that sixth game ended, people were making it an instant classic, talking about it as maybe the greatest game in World Series history. Of course, there was still the 7th game to be played for all the marbles. In 1975, the Boston Red Sox had made a miraculous comeback to win a sixth game, but then they lost the championship the next day. That's the precedent that was going through Tony's mind before he even hit the showers after the Cardinals' Game 6 celebration. And he pretty much verified that with his comments on his retirement day, in which he described his mind-set after Game 6 and before the decisive Game 7:

> *The first job that we have today is putting yesterday aside to be remembered later.*

Winning a game like that — it's harder, especially the signifi-cance. I mean, it's really hard. I can't imagine it being harder.

So since I'm one of the ones on the staff that gives that mes-sage, as soon as I got stirring (the morning after Game 6, the morning of Game 7), I refused to think about last night.

You control your mind. That's what we're trying to do as a team . . . this is a dead-even competition, and you cannot be dis-tracted by last night.

That's the true mark of a champion — forgetting the last vic-tory and preparing for the next one. And that one comment should be on every coach's wall:

The first job that we have today is putting yesterday aside to be remembered later. (Tony LaRussa, World Series Champion 2011)

A personal example: We beat No. 1–ranked North Carolina in the regional round of the 1984 NCAA tournament. It was a great win for our kids. The game wasn't over until 11:30 on a Thursday night, we didn't get through the post-game obliga-tions and back to our hotel until 2 a.m., and we had to play Virginia at noon on Saturday, with a chance to go to the Final Four. That was probably the hardest thing I've ever tried to do: Get our team back into the frame of mind to play "The Game after North Carolina."

I didn't get that done. We just weren't able to get from the last game into the next game. There were other uncontrollable factors, including irresponsible scheduling by the NCAA, but my job was to make sure my team "put yesterday aside to be remembered later" and focused on the next game. The scoreboard said we didn't do that well enough.

There's a business analogy here too in the boom-and-bust of the Internet start-ups which occurred around the year 2000. Many small technology companies were trying to emulate the success of AOL and others that had gotten very fast traction and rolled up huge windfalls for their young founders. Of course, most of these companies weren't earning much money (if any) and yet everyone got very cocky about the unlimited future.

Then, the market turned and suddenly the bottom fell out. The tech boom stalled and Wall Street took a bloodbath. This was the problem that caution and skepticism might have prevented. When you start gloating over your victories (or your profits), you're about to get your head handed to you. As one wise observer put it: "Early failure is usually better than early success, because the lesson in humility lasts a long time and makes you more effective over the long term."

I tried to teach my son Pat a lesson once when he was really young — maybe eight or nine — and he talked me into playing pool against him. He really had no chance given our respective skills, but I didn't like how carelessly he was playing, so I finished him off pretty fast. He started to rack the balls up to play again, and I just walked away, saying, "No, Pat, I don't want to play any more until you get better. Sometimes in sports or life, you just get one shot at it and you'd better be ready. You sure weren't ready today."

Several weeks later, we played again, and Pat actually beat me. I was stunned. I thought we were just starting an hour or so of playing, but he turned, walked up the stairs, and said, "No, Dad, sometimes you just get one chance." Lesson learned!

Don't Start Bad Habits

Some things that become very bad habits should be eliminated before they begin. And I don't mean only in basketball.

For example: How *can* people continue to smoke with all the medical evidence of cancer risk and lung damage? The "It won't happen to me" delusion is my idea of the highest form — and demonstrated risk — of positive, illusory thinking. Drinking to drunkenness is another thing society tolerates and I can't fathom. Drug use is another. Applying the term "social" or "recreational" to drug use sickens me. And the phrase "everybody does it" is a strong candidate as the most repulsive combination of words in the English language.

I can't say smokers or drinkers are radically different — or dumber—than the long list of people (that at times has included me) who eat their way to obesity. All those things have a starting point. That's where The Power of Negative Thinking can serve its greatest purpose.

KNIGHT'S NUGGETS,
THE PERILS OF POSITIVE THINKING:

Look at this restaurant! No cars! Easy parking, and we'll get served right away!

> *Ever notice how often restaurants with bad food do have lots of room to park?*

A picture is worth a thousand words.

> *Said, I'm guessing, by a lousy writer or an illiterate.*

The boss won't mind if I'm a little late.

> *What do you suppose this pink slip means?*

2

What Is There about the Word No?

I HAVE TWO CANDIDATES for the greatest words in the English language:

No. Don't.

And whatever you learned to the contrary in grammar class, there is a time for doubling up negatives, using both those great negatives at once.

I've had players I've told over and over and over again, *No, that is not what we want.* The words *"no"* and *"don't"* are important parts of the power of negative thinking, along with a whole long list of imperatives just as firm and final. I couldn't begin to tell you how many times I said to a player: What is there about the word "no" that you don't understand? What is there about the word "don't" that you don't understand?

Don't and *can't* are obviously negative phrases, but putting the words into use can bring very positive results. There is absolutely nothing wrong with saying "I can't." Ed Pillings, a great athletic trainer who served at Army under Col. Earl "Red" Blaik during his outstanding football years and later helped break me in as a head coach, told me a story that underlines the value of "I can't" in the right circumstances.

Col. Blaik, whom I got to know well during my West Point years, probably never had a player he thought more of than Pete Dawkins, who won the 1958 Heisman Trophy, joining Doc Blanchard and Glenn Davis as Blaik and Army's three Heisman winners. Pete was as tough as he was good, but a leg injury put him out for a time. Ed Pillings had him working on a device to build up the leg, and it was all he could do to manage the work. Col. Blaik watched, then moved in to offer some extra incentive: "Harder, Pete, harder. *Harder!*"

Pete already was giving it everything he had, and he finally snapped, "Dammit, Colonel, I *can't.*"

Blaik wasn't a coach anyone talked back to. But he knew his player. He nodded and walked away. "I can't" from Pete Dawkins meant he just damned well couldn't, and both men were smart enough to know it made no sense to go beyond that.

As with Pete Dawkins farther down the recovery path,

there might be a time when you are in position to do something later, but "I can't" is the best possible conclusion to reach about yourself when foolish optimism and determination are, at best, counterproductive.

You have to develop enough common sense to know what you can't do and focus on what you can. Know your limits. If you can't do it, don't, and say so, as Pete Dawkins did.

Injuries aren't the only thing that can be a reality check. Ability—or lack of it—needs a clear-eyed assessment too, whether you're thinking about yourself or as a coach or director you're thinking of someone else. One of the obligations as a coach is to make your players know their own strengths and weaknesses as well as those of their teammates. That's how teams win: by playing to their strengths and away from weaknesses. I made this into a simple doctrine: The shooters shoot, the passers pass and everybody plays defense.

Kenny Rogers said it best with a simple refrain in a song:

You gotta know when to hold 'em . . .

Know when to fold 'em:

Giving Mary a Rest

Ed Pillings as a trainer was a great advisor during my West Point days. I have often told the story of my first game as a head coach, in the 1965–66 season opener at Princeton. In the locker room before sending the team out to play, I was trying to do all the things I thought a head coach should do. I called the team together to recite "The Lord's Prayer." We did, and as we headed up the steps to go out on the court, Ed came up behind me, put an arm on my shoulder and said, "For what it's worth, let me tell you: You and prayers just aren't a good mix."

We never did it again.

And I don't mean anything at all disrespectful about that. I have a problem with calling God into play for anything competitive — whether asking, or expecting, Him to take sides.

I'm familiar with the line from Paul in Philippians 4:13 — "I can do all things through Christ, who strengthens me" — and I don't think that advisory had anything to do with the mundane world of basketball, or any competitive sport.

The simple truth is no one can do all things. Period. Bringing God into expectations, particularly into competition where one person's victory is another person's defeat, seems to me to be crossing a do-unto-others line. So when I hear a guy after a game-winning home run say or gesture that it happened because God was on his side, I think to myself, "He's saying God screwed the pitcher?" I look around and see truly tragic things happening every day in the world and think He has a whole lot better things to do than dabble in sports and play favorites.

I did have a player who made the sign of the cross before every free throw. I told him to quit it—not because the act offended me; he was a lousy shooter and I told him he was giving the church a bad name.

I also told a Catholic school football coach one time at his banquet to get Hail Mary out of his backfield and give her a rest: "You'll be a lot better off working to win games on your own with blocking and tackling than counting on pulling them out with desperation passes and divine help."

Once at Indiana I did take a priest with me to Notre Dame and sat him behind our bench for a game against the Irish. But I did it because Father Jim Higgins was a big fan, a great guy, and a personal friend of mine and a lot of our players, not because I thought priestly prayers were going to help us—especially at Notre Dame. If it came down to support by the clergy, we were going to be outpriested a thousand to one.

Challenging the Platitudes with One Word: Why?

My list of the most irritating platitudes starts with someone looking at a very messy situation and saying nonchalantly, "Oh, well, the sun will come up tomorrow." My response: Yeah, and it will flash brand-new daylight on the same old mess unless something is done to clean it up. I always feel like firing back at the sun-believers, "It's not God's dependability that's the question here; it's yours."

The one-word question to keep in mind when these mind-less, optimistic paeans to patience are thrown around is: Why?

"Everything will be better tomorrow."

Why?

"Everything will work out for the best."

Why?

"We'll get 'em next time." Why? You've apparently lost this time, so the evidence up to now certainly doesn't say that there will be a reversal of fortune. If there's a good, reasonable answer to that one-word question, then you're making prog-ress. If you're not, why not?

That simple challenge — "Why?" — is as important as a one-word question can get. Never hesitate to ask it — especially of yourself.

Attention Must Be Paid

One set of words that can make a huge difference in avoiding hasty decisions with nasty, unintended consequences is what I call the "shun" family. If you apply these words before you leap into a decision, then you will have much less "buyers' re-morse" no matter whether you're buying swamp land in Ari-zona or putting together a marketing plan in brand manage-ment. Here is the list of shuns:

Prevention

Hesitation

Correction

Suspicion

Attention

Recognition

Reservation(s)

Anticipation

Revelation

Organization

Dedication

Education

Caution

Rejection

Preparation

Gumption

There's probably a cousin or two I've left out. Maybe I've overlooked them, but I certainly haven't meant to shun them.

Can't and Don't on a Practical Level

Let's take on a little digest of things that I considered vital to my way of coaching and see how many would work as well in an office or around a kitchen table when life-shaping decisions are being made. As an example, while I'm talking really technical basketball for a moment, make your own applications to general life on how *don't* and *can't* fit into more practical experiences of learning and teaching.

On offense alone: A major part of my coaching was getting across the idea that—just as the great Chinese general Sun Tzu said—"A military operation involves deception." In sports, we improve almost every offensive move we make by setting it up with a false move first, a fake, or a reverse. As coaches, as leaders, we achieve that deception by saying over and over again on the practice floor, *No*, we *can't* make that kind of move without a fake first.

For instance: No, *don't* throw up an important shot without thinking about a shot fake. Without the fake, you're probably going to be shooting under pressure. Use the shot fake and you might draw a foul, or wind up with a one-dribble move to a wide-open shot. Using the shot fake and fake pass are reasons why we win, and not utilizing them is often the reason why we lose.

Now, granted, deception works much better in military

and sports arenas than in normal business boardrooms, but there is a carryover principle into business of game-planning any significant new action with well-thought-out preparation, self-discipline, and a little poker-faced deception where necessary. There's no need to put your best offer forward in a negotiation; let the other side reveal its intention. By faking a shot in basketball, you're forcing your opponents to show their hand first.

By the same token, you have to be wary of the first moves from the other side. Almost every first encounter in business with a potential partner is cordial and often lubricated with alcohol. The back-of-the-napkin approach seems to make perfect sense. "We'll be partners" — that's the operating principle — and "We'll let the lawyers work out the details."

In my playbook, you had better be on guard when things look *too* easy. Some basketball coaches, the ones who focus on building player confidence, like to teach, *When you think you're open, shoot.* Or: *When you think you've got a good shot, take it.*

I'm the kind of coach who holds up the red flag. Many players have a looser interpretation of "open" than I do, and think every shot is a good shot. They've got to be taught what for *them* is a good shot within their comfort and ability zone. The great pro players, since Jerry West and John Havlicek in my day to the very best today, can make just about anything they try in a key situation, but lesser players need to be more cautious. Talent and opportunity must mesh in the same way among office employees or staffs of salesmen. As a sales rep trying to win the big year-end bonus, is the deal you're about to close really good long-term for your company, or are you setting a precedent where executives back in the office will be dealing with other angry customers later who are demanding the same deal?

I teach my teams all kinds of principles in ball-handling that essentially say look before acting, know the situation you're creating. For example, the guards who bring the ball up the court have a tendency to make their first pass to a teammate on the baseline in the corner. My instruction is: *Don't pass the ball to the baseline unless the receiver has an open shot.* Why? If you pass to a man who's guarded down there, he may be trapped by a good defense and it can be hard to get the ball back out.

The same logic applies to working the ball into the center or post man. My caveat: *Don't pass to the post man unless you consider how tightly he's being guarded.* We want our post man to get the ball as often as we can because he has the shot closest to the basket, but the passer has to be taught how to do that. A high straight pass is easy to knock away or intercept, whereas a fake and then a bounce pass is safer, especially if the center can shield the incoming ball with his body.

These are all simple, logical rules of play that start with a negative — *never* risking that precious possession of the basketball. The smart, cautious athlete is doing in a split second what an investor may have to do in the split second of watching a stock market tape — consider the risks, calculate the best alternative, and then commit to it totally. All the initial negatives are processed instantly so that the ultimate choice is the right one — namely in basketball, getting the ball to someone closer to the basket for a higher percentage shot. I hope your stockbroker operates the same way — ruling out the risky moves and finding the low-hanging fruit that has the highest percentage of success. (Of course, I like the investment contrarians who don't follow the crowd when stock prices have become inflated. This is another example of "negative" judgment that leads to very positive results in your portfolio.)

Know When to Fold 'Em

One of the toughest situations for any leader or coach or investment advisor is letting go of a bad decision that you don't want to rescind because you made it. Corporations tend to have cultures that are very self-reinforcing, which means they resist products and ideas that are "not invented here." Likewise, individuals in authority tend to build their decision-making around their personal prejudices or their past experiences, which can be very dangerous.

Elimination of ideas that have outlived their utility is essential to almost any process of growth and achievement. Sometimes that means eliminating things that were once thought to be worthwhile — something, maybe, that you yourself once taught. No successful person, no thinking person, continues to do something that isn't working just because it was his or her idea.

Perseverance is an admirable trait, and one that can be positive when driven by the right kind of passion. But driving that passion into a ditch is pure stupidity. Thus, be smart and admit it when an investment decision has turned sour. Continuing to plow money into a bad investment — the cliché is "throwing good money after bad" — only makes it a worse investment, magnified by stupidity. The same logic applies in poker when you try to keep bluffing through bad hands. The stupidity multiplies and costs much more when an investment wastes time and effort, as well as money. Then stubborn perseverance becomes a double-edged sword that stabs you in the back. The smart "negative" thinker applies the same skepticism continually to every investment that he should have applied on the first day making the decision. The successful person has to be able to change his mind when something isn't working and try to bail out or possibly find a more creative solution.

Of course, playing poker offers you the opportunity to hold

'em or fold 'em on every hand, whereas life doesn't present such easy options. Kenny Rogers said it best with a simple refrain in a song.

For a more sophisticated corollary to Kenny Rogers, when you're not playing poker, you have to work harder and let perseverance work in your favor. For instance, take the wisdom of the Oak Ridge Boys, on the best way to satisfy a thirst:

Dig a little deeper in the well, boys,
Dig a little deeper in the well.
If you want a good cool drink of water,
You gotta dig a little deeper in the well.

My daddy used to tell me don't be fooled by what you see;
If you want to get to the heart of things, you gotta look
  way down deep.
Second place don't get it, son, winners got to come in first.
There's nothin' worse than to take a drink that leaves you
  with a thirst.

The art of coaching is moving away from the game plan when things aren't working in the course of the game. Maybe it's a time-out or a substitution that can change the momentum. That's holding or folding your cards as needed. But the greater wisdom is in the second refrain because if you have a team that's thirsty and you've prepared them by digging deeper into their resolve and by giving them the tools to limit their mistakes, then your teams have a better chance to wind up in the win column.

The same is true in business. Corporate "strategy" — a favorite business school buzzword — is really very simple. It means deploying your assets (and your people) in ways that are the most advantageous given the resources at hand. We now call our personnel departments "Human Resources" because we recognize that any organization has employees who are key to its success. Here's that negative warning signal: The term "resources" also means that there is a limit to the human talent involved, and thus focus is important, so you don't squander those resources on foolish sideshows.

That's why as a coach I always tried to cut away the mistakes, because each time we had the ball was a limited resource, and we needed to get it in the basket without wasting the chance to take the shot. For the player, knowing when to hold that ball or pass it or shoot it required stripping away the crowd noise or the opponent's hand in his face and making the right call almost instinctively. Behind that instinct were the days and weeks of practice in building up a "muscle memory" of what to do next — and what not to do.

The well-prepared and well-trained player could hear Kenny Rogers singing in his head.

For the coach or leader, the strategy is knowing how to use your personnel and knowing how you *can't*. Know when you've got everything going your way, and know also when things aren't going the way you want and you have to make some adjustments. Know when to hold them, know when to fold them.

Know when to walk away, know when to run. Realize when what you are doing isn't going to enable you to win this game. If things are really going bad, get out of it, *now!* You've got to have something else planned. If this doesn't work, then . . .

If . . . then . . . is another coupling, a big, big factor in sports and in life. If A happens, then go to B. If B doesn't work, we have to be ready with a C, and a D, and an E. We have to have an *if . . . then . . .* plan to everything we are doing.

One Other Thing to Remember

Competition is never static. Don't think that the guy you're competing against isn't planning, and creating alternative plans so that he can get his team or business in the best possible position to win. You have to recognize when what you're doing isn't working and get out of it.

When you don't have the hands-down best — team, product, talent, whatever — what will separate you from the rest starts with preparation. Luck can win sometimes, but preparation is a more consistent formula for success. Good teams can get lucky and win, bad teams can't. Don't fall for any platitudes about "we tried hard." If you prepare properly with a reasonable amount of talent, you can win. The object is to win, fairly and by the rules, but winning nonetheless.

Less Hope, More Sweat

I started playing basketball when I was twelve years old, and my whole life since then has either been playing it or coaching it or watching it. I'm not sure I "know" anything else. But it has taught me one thing: There is a hell of a difference between winning and losing. Winning is a product of good leadership. Leadership is getting people out of their comfort zone.

We all have a comfort zone. We like to be able to play or work at a certain pace. A leader has to know when that pace is not good enough. One of the things I always tried to do in October and November was get my team out of its comfort zone and into working at getting better, as individual players and as a team.

Negative thinking—realizing that an average game from your team and average preparation from you isn't likely to beat an average game by the very good team you're about to play—can give you by far your best chance to win that game.

Positive thinking that amounts to sheer hope isn't going to

do it. There is the cliché "Hope springs eternal," but not within me. My feeling is that today, way too often, hope has replaced sweat. To win that game, you'd better make sure that your team, and you, are doing some sweating.

When you're a coach saying to yourself, "Boy, the information I'm getting is that this next opposing team is awfully good," the next thing you should think is: "*We* have to be at *our* best. We've got to plan a little bit differently here. We can't do what we normally do and beat this team." Nor can we count on tricky plays that might backfire. Whatever we put together for a game plan — any game plan, especially when we see very little margin for error — we're counting most on *our* execution being better than theirs.

In a normal game, I never wanted my players to think, "We're okay because we have better players and we're favored to win." I wanted their feeling of being ready to play to come from thinking that our planning was better, our preparation was better. My job was to make sure that it was. I also wanted them to know that even if well prepared, we had to execute as well as we could to beat this other team. I wanted to plan every game as though it was against a good opponent, because it was. I felt every time we played, the real opponent was the game itself — how close could we come to playing it perfectly?

I *have* told my teams, "Boys, the only way we can lose to

this team is . . .", and here again it becomes *if . . . then . . . If* we don't do the things we have worked on for this game, *then* we get beat. That kind of negative approach has a corollary so obvious it doesn't even have to be said: *If* we do these things, *then* we win. But I always wanted them to be wary, to be motivated, and to realize that winning starts with the "negative" . . . *if we don't. . . .*

Negative Imaging: If We Don't . . .

The point is the negative thinker always knows there is a chance that he can get beat, so he works to make that as unlikely as he can. The coach, caught up with visioning good things and with "positive imaging," risks having the real possibility of losing never even enter his mind. So he has a tendency to overlook problems he needs to prepare for.

I prefer negative imaging—*if . . . then . . .* "*If* we don't do these things, *then* sure as hell we're gonna get beat." And "*If* we do have the right approach, the right preparation, and we play as well as we can, *then* we have a chance to win."

The *if . . . then . . .* model is built on information. Understanding precisely what the "if" means, what the team has to do or avoid doing, is critical. One of the most important statements a coach can make to himself is: *I don't know, but I'm going to find out.*

Asking questions is the essence of learning. In the daily

challenge of trying to be a manager, every leader has blind spots, just as a quarterback will have blind spots when he is being rushed by 300-pound linemen. For a coach, it's critical to try to figure out what you might be missing; for instance, what the video you're reviewing is not telling you.

A coach — a leader — cannot be afraid to admit to himself or others: *I don't know.* The positive guy is prone to say: I'm sure of this, or this is the way it is. The cautious guy who has the best chance to win is always going to be the one who says: I'm not sure, I don't know. Knowing what you don't know is one of the most important lessons in life. That's why you have assistant coaches or trusted associates who can help you find out.

There is a credo that journalists follow which is a favorite of mine:

> *I have had six honest serving men.*
> *They taught me all I knew.*
> *Their names are*
> *What, Where, When,*
> *How, Why, and Who.*

There isn't always an absolute right way and a wrong way to do things, but there usually is a better way, a high-percentage way. The positive thinker generally feels that his way will be the right way and nothing will go wrong, if he just *believes*. The negative thinker *disbelieves*. He takes every precaution to prevent the wrong thing from happening, and in doing so has a much better chance of things turning out right in the end.

Rudyard Kipling: First of the "If . . . Then" Guys?

I think Rudyard Kipling was an *if . . . then . . .* guy, and his classic poem "If" includes some of the most profound thoughts along those lines — the "then" is omitted, yes, but pretty clearly implied.

Segments of the poem I particularly liked:

> *If you can keep your head when all about you*
> *Are losing theirs and blaming it on you;*
> *If you can trust yourself when all men doubt you,*
> *But make allowance for their doubting, too;*
>
> *If you can dream — and not make dreams your master;*
> *If you can think — and not make thoughts your aim,*
> *If you can meet with Triumph and Disaster*
> *And treat those two impostors just the same;*
>
> *. . . If you can force your heart and nerve and sinew*
> *To serve your turn long after they are gone;*

And so hold on when there is nothing in you
Except the Will which says to them "hold on!"

If you can fill the unforgiving minute
With sixty seconds' worth of distance run,
Yours is the Earth and everything that's in it,
And — which is more — you'll be a Man, my son!

Wow!

Kipling would have been a hell of a coach.

The Best I've Seen

I'm inclined to think that Johnny Bench must have been the greatest catcher ever to put on a baseball uniform. I think Michael Jordan is the all-time greatest basketball player. I like to think Ted Williams was the greatest, purest hitter. But like just about everybody else, I tend to think the best ever is the best *I've* ever seen, and that realization stands out to me every time I hear some guy in a newspaper or behind a microphone establishing a play by a shortstop — say a Luis Aparicio, or an outfield catch, even the one by Willie Mays off Vic Wertz in the 1954 World Series — as the absolute greatest ever . . . without a doubt! I hear that, shake my head, and think, "Son, you never even *saw* so-and-so . . . or so-and-so."

This must have been going on with human beings for quite

a while now, because a Roman poet named Lucretius wrote in the century before Christ:

> *A fair-sized stream seems vast to one who until then*
> *Has never seen a greater; so with trees, with men.*
> *In every field each man regards as vast in size*
> *The greatest objects that have come before his eyes.*

Before *his* eyes. There were human beings doing remarkable things before you or I or the oldest and wisest among us ever existed. Lucretius should be posted in every broadcasting booth and press box as a warning.

"Sports Intelligence" Is Not a Gimme

I never felt I could take it for granted that even our best players had learned on their own to be good thinkers. Maybe that's why great players are rarely great coaches: because what they do instinctively, they assume other guys — smart basketball players — will do instinctively, too. It doesn't always work that way.

I coached from a negative standpoint, right from even the best incoming players' first practice: Okay, these kids have good athletic skills and generally really know how to play the game — except they usually come to the college level with an offensive mindset, and they haven't been required by their coach to play much defense, for fear of fouling out.

I found that a kid who is a great scorer more often than not has the innate skills to be a good defensive player. One of the best selling points for improving a player's defense is simply noticing when that player makes progress. When your players show you they are really working to improve their skills in any phase of the game, that's the time you have to encourage them, so they know their work is being noticed. That's another basic tenet of leadership: Always criticize sloppy play and praise good performance.

Another factor that bedevils major college coaches is that the kind of players recruited at an elite college level in high school normally made their teams so strong that they weren't in a whole lot of tight situations. I felt my job was to teach them to think — to read situations and react properly.

I did factor in general intelligence very strongly when recruiting — and I always had a lot of smart kids to work with. But in college they were stepping up a level. I wanted them to realize — to understand — that they had a lot to learn, that they had to do things the way I wanted them done. Frankly, there was one right way — my way. We had to work at doing things instinctively that enabled us to win, and eliminate the sloppiness or risky play that could beat us in a close game.

We had to work at doing things that enabled us to win, and eliminate the sloppiness or risky plays that could beat us in a close game.

If you're the one in charge, on a basketball court or in an office, that's a paragraph you need to read again and again. In the corporate world, I know many executives who shun recruiting at the so-called "elite" business schools because the students come out of there thinking they're trained and ready to be CEOs. I personally liked recruiting kids who might be from lesser-known schools where they had been through some hard knocks and were ready to roll up their sleeves and learn to cast off bad habits. The athletes from poor families could perhaps recall their parents working double shifts and two jobs so that the family could survive. These kids were focused on what it took because they knew basketball could be a ticket to success later in life.

I wanted to make our players play better because they "thought" better and reacted better than the other team did — and to take pride in having that edge on their side in game-deciding situations.

If you, as the head coach, can teach your team to think under pressure, to react well to changes, then you don't have to have as much talent as the other teams. We're back to positive-negative.

Once again, mine is a negative approach.

I can't accept these players for what they are on the surface when they arrive. The positive coach says: I've got great players, we are going to be fine, and all I have to do is not screw this up. I have never felt that way. I felt, *Okay, we have enough talent to be good.* But long ago in coaching I developed the adage: *The mental is to the physical as four is to one.* If I can teach our players how to win the mental game, we're going to have our very best shot at winning.

It's not automatic that teams play smart every night. A couple of seasons ago, Brent Musburger and I were doing a game on ESPN between Kansas State and Baylor, two highly regarded teams. That night neither team was playing with intelligence. During the first half, Brent said, "Coach, you're a big baseball fan. Do you remember when Casey Stengel asked, 'Can't anyone here play this game?'" A great line. Toward the end of the game, after another sequence of poor plays, I said, "Brent, when I go to sleep tonight I'm going to pause and say thank you, for all the really smart players I had."

Don't Stop for Time-Outs

Once our players were trained to think, there was one consistent indication of my trust in them. During games, I usually left them on their own to play through tough situations without calling time-out.

A friend told me once, "When you get to heaven, the first thing Saint Peter is going to dump on you is a whole boatload of unused time-outs." We must have led the world in those.

That wasn't altogether a demonstration of trust. Sometimes my intent was more of a teaching step. As the season went along, I wanted our players — individually and as a team — to have developed an ability to think and work their own way through tough stretches on the floor.

When the other team was on a run, another announcer I like and respect a lot, Dick Vitale, would be screaming, *"Gotta take a T-O, Bobbee!"* We often didn't. Usually we didn't just for that very reason: teaching our players to think — to reach down into what we had been stressing on the practice floor since day one and apply those negative reminders, the "if we don't" principles. If I didn't see improvement pretty quickly, *then* I'd take that time-out. And I will tell Saint Peter, in the long run, I think that my philosophy won us a whole lot more games than his would have. (I know there are a few cynics out there who say the only way Saint Peter and I will get together is if he comes down and takes a boat ride on the River Styx.)

There was one exception to my general theory of not rushing to take time-outs, and that was tournament play. The

NCAA "March Madness" is a single-loss elimination event, so you must win to keep advancing. There's nothing more final than a tournament loss. I always tried to keep all game preparation as normal as possible in tournaments, but if things started slipping then a quick time-out made sense. In general, however, my theory was that if you made your ideas clear enough in practice, then you didn't need a time-out to reinforce them. And even more important: Don't try to make a brilliant change when things are going well.

The Last-Shot Time-Out

An even more significant and consistent indication of my trust in my players was that they knew in the final seconds of a tensely contested game I didn't want them to do what everyone else does: Take a time-out to go over what we wanted to do, set up a play . . .

No! If you suddenly get possession, time is running out, and we must have a basket, you should *know in advance* what we want to do: If you have time, run our offense to get the best shot you can get. If you have to strike fast, go up-court immediately and use the broken floor to your advantage. Do *not* stop the clock and let them set up their defense. You have the ball, your team has the collective intelligence, everyone's in transition — attack!

This credo won us a lot of games, including one national championship. And it brought me a compliment I've always cherished because of how much I respected the source. After we went from a defensive rebound to the game-winning basket without taking a time-out in our 1987 final game with Syracuse, the great TV sports announcer Curt Gowdy shook my hand and said: "You're the only coach I've ever known who would have done that with a national championship on the line."

Having guts is one thing. I also had really smart players. When the chips were down, I believed they would do the right thing because that's what they were taught to do.

The time to make substantive in-game changes is halftime. The positive thinker counts on a "Don't panic" philosophy—"we're all right, we've got 20 minutes to go in this game." Hey, it hasn't been all right thus far, and it probably won't be unless we make some changes. The ability to adjust, to make changes from what you originally set out to do, is critically important. Staying with something that isn't working simply isn't in the cards for the negative thinker. *Knowing when to walk away, knowing when to run,* hey, time out, we've got to change the game plan, make some substitutions. Turn things around. *Adjust* is another of those invaluable leadership words.

Digging Deeper and Finding Rewards

If you're going against a really good team, maybe even a more talented team—in business, a bigger, better-known, better-financed company—you'd better have something a little different in your plans. The late Steve Jobs of Apple is a classic example of a leader who didn't have the resources of rival Microsoft, but he learned the hard way (after being fired) and came back with a vision that worked.

One important negative step was eliminating the dozens of models that Apple was producing and focusing on a sleeker and smaller number of products that were easier to brand and sell. He was a perfectionist who certainly knew the lesson of digging deeper in the well. He also believed that by controlling all aspects of the manufacturing process—rather than licensing it out to other manufacturers—you eliminate the flaws and bugs that are the curse of software design.

Now, I know I've said that desire alone can't win games. But it's an invaluable asset. In the final minutes of close games, when one play can swing everything and your team has played hard and left everything out on the court just to get to this point, there isn't a coach in America who hasn't looked into exhausted eyes in a huddle and said, "Now's the time we've got to dig down deep and play as well as we can—with no mistakes." *Dig a little deeper in the well, boys.* I can't tell you how many times some great kids did exactly that for one of our teams.

Dangers of Overconfidence

I don't doubt that both the positive and negative thinkers can each have a very strong will to win. Both *want* to win.

But the positive thinker who has a great will to win is prone to give determination too big a role in his thinking. Determination determines a lot less than preparation does.

"Confidence" is not one of my favorite words.. Too many times confidence is a false feeling that you have before you really understand the situation. Custer's Last Stand is history's illustration.

The negative-conscious person has a great opportunity to capitalize on how vulnerable a lot of people are because of their illusory positive thinking about things they don't understand or actions they are incapable of performing. The positive-thinking basketball player is sure he can throw a pinpoint pass between two defenders, or "I've missed three shots in a row—I'm due!" And another clunker goes up. "Everything's going to turn out all right." Why?

Positive thinking can lead people into believing there's *nothing* they're not capable of doing well, if they visualize doing it well. Both Michael Phelps and Mark Spitz — who was a great swimmer at Indiana when I started there — could visualize swimming faster than everyone else because each was one of the most talented athletes ever to jump in a pool. For the rest of us, *very* few people are capable of doing everything their job or aspirations require. Knowing their own deficiencies has enabled a lot of people to make their greatest strides toward success.

Insecurity can have intangible benefits. Being able to self-analyze and be self-critical is very important. You can accomplish surprising things if you ask questions and consult others about areas where you need to improve. Realizing your shortcomings takes an awareness. It's laughable, but there are positive guys who go right ahead thinking they have all the answers because of some divine gift — "Holiday Inn Express" guys who have seen something done easily so it won't be any problem. Here's another don't: Don't be reluctant to pluck the fruits of victory right out of those people's hands.

Know Thyself

Understanding limitations — your players' or your own — is the first step toward overcoming them. I heard once about a man in his eighties who had mastered an art I admire: fly-rod casting. It never left him. Well up in years, he could wade into a stream and, with a perfect snap of the wrist, make a cast to exactly the spot he wanted, his grace and ease unfailingly causing younger witnesses to marvel at what an athlete he must have been.

Once he was standing onshore casting out into the water when he heard a voice from somewhere close say: "Pick me up." His hearing hadn't stayed with him as well as his casting had, so after looking around and seeing no one, he went back to casting, and he heard the voice again: "I said *pick me up. I'm down here. By your feet." He looked down and saw a huge frog.

"Pick me up, kiss me, and I'll turn into the most beautiful woman you've ever seen. You'll be indulged with pleasures no man has ever dreamed of, for the rest of your life. You'll . . ."

He picked the frog up, looked at it a second, and put it in the pocket of his fishing jacket.

"Hey!" the frog screamed. "Didn't you *hear* me? I said kiss me, and I'll turn into a beautiful woman, and for the rest of your life give you pleasures no man has ever known."

He went back to casting.

The voice screamed again: "Didn't you HEAR me?! I said KISS ME and . . ."

His arm arched another perfect cast, and without looking down he interrupted: "That may be . . . but at my age, I'd rather have a talking frog."

KNIGHT'S NUGGETS

I don't care what the weatherman said, it doesn't even feel like rain.

Umbrellas aren't all that expensive, compared to pneumonia.

You can't always believe that gauge. I know there's plenty of gas to get us home.

Remind him of that when he's walking two miles in snow to find a station.

Don't worry, Dad. This test is going to be easy.

Better idea, Son: Study.

3

A Limit to Negativism

T HE LEADER — of a basketball team, a business, whatever — must set standards high but always be quick to recognize good performance — good within the scope of what that individual is physically or mentally capable of doing.

The coach and the leader must recognize that his players and his team are never going to be good at things they are just not physically equipped to do. They can improve as players or as a team, but almost always there are some physical or maybe even mental limitations that they are just not going to be able to overcome with all the determination, the willpower, in the world.

As a player, recognize what you're good at, what you *can* do, and get as good as you can at it. But at the same time, recognize what you *don't* do well now, but can with work, and—as important as anything—what you simply cannot do, now or ever. All the willpower in the world won't lift an average high jumper over the bar at seven feet. As a leader, you have to help people recognize and understand that—yourself first of all.

Now, I may surprise you with this thought. Amid all those firm negatives that bring things into line, a coach or any other kind of leader should never overlook a chance to be positive.

Sure, I'm an example there. My wife, Karen, was the best person possible for me to run things by, because she has a great understanding of the game of basketball, as good as anybody I have ever known in any sport. One of the things she constantly warned me about was being *too* negative—teaching the right way, the best way, to do things, but not taking away from kids the idea of being the best *they* can be. And the leader, in this case me, should always be quick to praise them when they do things the right way.

Vitally important in working with people is to recognize and emphasize how good someone is at the things he or she does best. "You are invaluable to our team when this is what you are doing, but when you start deviating from what you are really good at, then you become more of a liability than an asset." It is not a disgrace to be *really* good at one thing and not so good at another.

The recognition and elimination of what can't be done: that's the Power of Negative Thinking.

I have to laugh at the working acronym for that title: Power of Negative Thinking — PONT. I worked for three years at Indiana with John Pont, the football coach, and I've never met a bigger optimist in my life — great guy, terrific to be around, introduced me to some people who became valued and valuable friends in breaking me in at Indiana. And boy, what an optimist!

People just like John are why I don't want this to be considered a war on optimists per se. John died at eighty in 2008, and I loved the guy. We'd have never met if he hadn't been such an optimist, because schools like Indiana would never have a football coach if there weren't people out there who look at situations and see hope where all evidence says success is unlikely.

John actually made it work for a while. In 1967, his third year at Indiana, coming off 2–8 and 1–8–1 seasons, he put together a team buoyed by an unsung senior defense and sparked by sophomores on offense — irrepressible kids at the headlined positions who hadn't been conditioned to lose. By continual one- and two- and three- or four-point margins, they strung together eight straight wins starting out the season, getting just enough points — frequently in the very last seconds — for that stout, almost unnoticed defense to combine with them for wins. From nowhere they crashed the Top 10 and capped their season by upsetting one of rival Purdue's best teams ever to go to the Rose Bowl — the only time in Indiana history that has happened.

At Pasadena, home of the Rose Bowl, this whole PONT thing, this Power of Negative Thinking idea, actually came up, and it was optimist John who brought it up.

Naturally, he was the darling of the West Coast press when he and his team arrived for the weeklong lead-up to the game. At one of the press sessions, John was asked how, with that Indiana history of losing in football, he had convinced those young offensive stars of his to come to a place like Indiana.

"I told them the truth," John said. "'You can go other places and win, yes. But if you come here and do it, you'll go down in history. You'll be all-time heroes — the names associated with Indiana's breakthrough.'"

"But John," a press guy said, "in essence you're saying 'Come join us *because* we haven't won.' How can you expect someone to buy anything that negative?"

John's smooth, classic answer: "They sell insurance every day."

Stop and think about that. That's exactly what insurance is: recognition that as positive as we all like to feel about ourselves and everything around us, the reality is that unexpected things do happen, and we'd better be prepared.

John made the unexpected happen.

And what he told those kids he brought to Bloomington turned out to be absolutely truthful. Talk about the Rose Bowl anywhere else in the Big Ten, and you have to be more specific — which year, which team? In Bloomington, Rose Bowl means one year, one team: that wild and wacky 1967 season. Period. And the names on that team *are* all-time heroes in Indiana football.

Tie in that little tale, and PONT isn't a bad-fitting acronym after all.

"PONT" in a Nutshell

There's one other phrase I love along these lines, and it came from Ronald Reagan, the president with the characteristic smile — the amiable fellow called the "Great Communicator," whose byword in diplomatic negotiations was: "Trust, but verify."

Now, that is my idea of the Power of Negative Thinking personified.

The Odds Are Against You

There is a certain racetrack optimism that can find its way into the real world. Betting on long shots is one example, whether they're bad horses or bad stocks. Yes, some come in and earn big paydays. But not often. There's a reason for those odds. Most of the time—the vast majority of the time, like fifty times out of fifty-one, as those 50–1 odds say—defying big odds with a bet or an investment is money thrown away.

And the follow-up advice that you won't hear only at the track—"Double up on the next one and get your money back"—is an almost-sure way for you to wind up twice as deep in the hole. (I prefer the adage *When you're in a hole, stop digging.*)

There's an old coaches' adage that I'll pass along because it applies here: Dumb plays are usually followed by dumber plays.

Dumb investments repeated are doubly dumb investments. With your bookie or your broker, never forget: *They* make money on the transaction, however things turn out—the story of all gambling. *You* gamble; the house never does, because it's playing the percentages times thousands of rolls of the dice.

Gambling odds persist even at the simplest level. Think all those Catholic bingo games were set up for Protestants to get rich? Or for that matter, parishioners?

P. T. Barnum's "There's a sucker born every minute" should be placed in the dictionary as the definition of the word *gambling.*

Gambling—the word, the practice—has a particular repugnance in college basketball. The biggest scandal in the history of the college game — biggest until the modern "one-and-done" travesty, anyway, but that's another subject — came before I was even a teenager: the point-shaving scandals that surfaced in New York in the early 1950s and mushroomed out to involve some of the biggest college basketball programs around the country.

I was a fifth grader in 1951. By then, my dad had already hammered home to me that gambling was one thing I was to stay away from — always. That thought never left me because he was so adamant on the subject, and then as my interest in basketball grew I knew what a bad word the whole subject of gambling had become in the college game. Then I moved into coaching and came into the metropolitan New York area with my West Point teams.

I met Clair Bee, whose brilliance as a coach made it my everlasting good fortune that I became as close to him as a son. A couple of his Long Island University players were implicated in that early-1950s scandal — not that Coach Bee himself or any coach was implicated, but all of those indicted players' coaches were shocked and disbelieving that such a thing could happen on their teams.

As closely as a coach watches everything that happens in a game, as great as some of those coaches were, *they* couldn't detect point-shaving — mainly because they couldn't imagine it, chalking up misplays to the damned-fool things players sometimes do in a game, even the best ones, crazy things . . . but intentionally.

Claire Bee and Joe Lapchick were New York college coaches whom I revered in my West Point days. Lapchick was coaching the New York Knicks during the scandal, but he had coaching stints at St. John's before and after that period, so he certainly knew college basketball. As the scandal unfolded, he saw the shambles. He maintained a scrapbook of newspaper clippings through his retirement in the late '60s. He would make it a practice of bringing out that scrapbook and showing it to his players every year as a warning of how easily everything good in their basketball lives could disappear.

When he died in 1970, his wife gave that scrapbook to me, because she said I was one of his favorites. I couldn't have received a more treasured memory of Coach Lapchick because I knew what the scrapbook meant to him.

All of that underlines how I feel about gambling. It was a great example of how, in my own upbringing, Father really did know best. When you gamble, you're a loser before the results are posted.

A True Specialist in Winning

Eras come and go in college basketball, but one little-noted but long-remembered player had a lasting effect on the way the game of basketball is played. And it wasn't a coach who did that: It was a modest star named Bill Russell.

Bill was a tall player who didn't shoot very well and got cut from his Oakland McClymonds High School team as a junior. But at the University of San Francisco, he led his team to the 1955 NCAA championship and, in the 1955–56 season, the first undefeated championship in NCAA history. In the process, he introduced to basketball the art of disciplined shot-blocking — not just lunging out of control toward a shot-taker, but reacting to a shot so quickly and so well that the ball was kept in play and reclaimed to start an offensive possession, frequently a fast break. Before Bill Russell, there wasn't even a column for blocked shots in a box score; there are no individual or team records for that skill prior to his arrival.

His height, strength, and timing also made him one of the greatest defensive rebounders ever to play the game, and he pioneered, in development of the outlet pass from the defensive board to start a fast break.

More than that, he played with an emphasis on winning — never focused on points, never on statistics — just on winning. And in that he is beyond everyone else's reach who ever played a team sport: starting with those two NCAA championships at San Francisco, carrying through a gold medal in the 1956 Olympics at Melbourne, and extending through eleven NBA championships. In a thirteen-year playing career with the Boston Celtics, Bill Russell was on teams that won fourteen major championships in fifteen years. Nobody else, in any sport, is close. And this by a guy who, in a game that idolizes its shooters, was not a great shooter — a great, great player, but not a great shooter.

Even Winning Has Risks

As focused as my coaching has been on winning, I know even *that* goal has its hazards. Success actually can be one of the biggest problems a coach or any leader has to deal with.

In April 2011, the *Harvard Business Review* devoted its entire monthly magazine to the subject of failure — obviously, the polar opposite of success. But, in an article in that issue titled "Why Leaders Don't Learn from Success," authors Francesca Gino and Gary P. Pisano cited something similar to Tali Sharot's "optimism bias." One of the major reasons success can produce negative long-term results is because of what they called "overconfidence bias":

> Success increases our self-assurance. Faith in ourselves is a good thing, of course, but too much of it can make us believe we don't need to change anything.

In the article, Gino and Pisano listed "overconfidence bias" as the second of three impediments that success can put in front of any enterprise.

The first is the inclination to make what psychologists call "fundamental attribution errors." When we succeed, we're likely to conclude that our talents and our current model or strategy are the reasons. We give short shrift to the part that . . . random events may have played.

And:

The third impediment is the "failure-to-ask-why syndrome" — the tendency not to investigate the causes of good performance systematically. When executives and their teams suffer from this syndrome, they don't ask the tough questions that would help them expand their knowledge or alter their assumptions about how the world works.

We almost always work at finding why we lost, or failed. Too rarely do coaches think about why they won, but it's an equally important, equally instructive question.

Why? I rest my case.

What, Me Worry?

Another publication, *Bottom Line Personal,* in its August 15, 2011, issue, shed a new light on what contributes to lifelong health. The issue's front-page lead story was headlined: "Worrying Helps You Live Longer."

Author Howard S. Friedman, a Ph.D. and distinguished

professor of psychology at the University of California–Riverside, cited "a groundbreaking eight-decade study that followed 1,528 Americans from early childhood through their deaths" and reported:

> Much of the common advice about living a long life — chill out and don't work too much — is *wrong*. . . . The study revealed that people who plan and worry tend to stay healthier and live longer than those who don't — and that hard work and the accompanying stress are actually good for you.
>
> Here's what really does extend life: conscientiousness.
>
> People who are detail-oriented, responsible, and organized live longer than those who aren't. . . . Conscientious people are more prudent in their personal habits. . . .
>
> It's a myth that people who are really cheerful tend to be healthier and live longer than those who view the world through a darker lens. In the study, people who were described by their parents as unusually cheerful and worry-free tended to die sooner than their less optimistic counterparts.
>
> You say worry, I say consider. You say conscientious, I say prudent. You say "Those with an excess of optimism may feel so invincible that they don't make reasonable precautions," I say you're right.

My career-long coaching philosophy, perfectly phrased. The guy who knows it all going into a game — or a test, or a challenge — usually forgets it all in the face of a crisis.

Let me put it this way:

Worry has lost a lot fewer games than over-confidence has.

Just Do the Job

We all risk getting to a point where, when successes come, we expect a pat on the back because we have done our job so well.

Stop and think about that. Aren't you *supposed* to do it well — as well as you possibly can?

I never asked for a raise after winning a tournament or conference championship. I also figured they wouldn't take anything away if we didn't.

I realized my thinking was out of line so long ago that I remember being shocked in reading that a college football coach's contract called for him to be paid more than $600,000. And if he won nine games, he would get $16,000 more. I thought, *What is he being paid the first $600,000 to do?*

We're not too far from seeing another zero added to that kind of contract — a salary ten times as high, $6 million a year; they're already above $5 million. And I'll bet even those $5 million contracts, as absurdly excessive as they are, also include a bonus for winning championships.

I'll repeat: *What the hell are they being paid a huge base salary to do?*

I won't even get into the contracts — and this is now common — that give extra thousands if the coach's *recruiting* class is ranked among the national leaders. Or if a certain percentage of kids from his team graduate.

When the first part — how self-styled experts ranked your recruits — and the last part — educating and graduating your players — ceased being an accepted part of the head coach's responsibility and stopped mattering to anyone with responsibility at all, I knew I had coached way too long.

That all comes into the point I was making about doing your job without waiting for pats on the back.

I always told my players: "Don't wait for *me* to pat you on the ass. Just worry about me booting you in the ass. Good things will happen to you if you play smart and play hard. You're not here on scholarship to lose. I didn't recruit you to lose. Losing is abnormal; losing is unusual; losing is unacceptable. That's not what we're here for. Playing as smart as we can play, and playing as hard as we can play — that's what we're here for. Winning comes from that, and that's acceptable."

I believed that.

KNIGHT'S NUGGETS

That light ahead stays on caution an extra-long time.

Not as long as a trooper's flashing light.

What a nice little dog.

And what mean teeth.

There's a motel down the road that always has rooms.

The word you need to learn is R-E-S-E-R-V-A-T-I-O-N-S.

Have faith that you'll be OK.

Get a good doctor.

4

History's Negatives, Starting with the Bible

I DON'T MEAN TO BE so bold as to line up God on the side of negative thinking. But have you ever realized that seven of the Ten Commandments start with *thou shalt NOT?* Thou shalt NOT murder, thou shalt NOT steal, thou shalt NOT commit adultery, thou shalt NOT covet — they're all right there.

And the three that don't could just as well have had the same structure.

Even beyond that, the first things we are taught by our parents are what not to do.

Don't cross the street without looking.

Don't go to bed without brushing your teeth.

Don't leave your fly unzipped.

Don't you dare miss the school bus.

Don't get in trouble with your teacher or you'll have double the trouble when you get home.

Thou shalt not works in later life, too. The first step toward getting a good job is eliminating reasons not to be hired. You get better gas mileage—and avoid paying fines, too—if you don't speed. And think how many lives would have been saved if there had been a decision to say "No!" to smoking before people got started on that terrible habit.

Thou Shalt Nots *Work in Leadership Too*

For anyone who wants to be a leader, here are Ten Commandments of my own:

    I. Don't accept status quo. Look for better when others are satisfied.

  II. Always question—the best of all questions: "Why?"

III. Always worry. If you can't think of a thing to be worried about, worry about being overconfident.

IV. Look for improvements to make in yourself or bad habits to break. Don't drink to excess or smoke at all, given the proven cancer risks.

   V. Don't act without evidence or buy something without checking thoroughly; before job interviews, eliminate all possible reasons not to be hired.

  VI. Be skeptical—untrusting. In every theory, look for proof. Verify, as President Reagan said.

 VII. Make your players or employees work to get better—encourage them, challenge them, maybe even inspire them to do it, but make it clear that the "same old, same old" is *not* acceptable. When they're saying "The boss is never satisfied," count it as a compliment. (I heard that one of my players once said, "He'll never be satisfied until we hit every shot and shut the other team out." He didn't know me well enough. They'd better all be A+ students, and never have thrown the ball away either.)

VIII. Never think talent alone will determine the outcome, whether it's your side versus the other side in a game or a competitive deal. Plan and train so that your side makes fewer mistakes.

  IX. Never talk too much. Get yourself a degree from the Shut-Up School and remember it when talking about your competitors, whether they're a sports team or a sales team. Self-promotion and gloating never have a place; let your products or your performance do the talking. I hate it when a coach or a player boasts about

71

his own team *before* a big game. That's an incentive to the other side.

X. Never stop looking for new ideas. Be self-critical of your beliefs when others offer possible alternatives. Remember, you're not the inventor of the wheel or the Internet. Learn from the wisdom of others — listen to people who came before, like the playwright George Bernard Shaw: "Some see things as they are and ask, 'Why?' I see things as they could be and ask, 'Why not?'"

Shaw would have been a hell of a CEO.

George Bernard Shaw also shared a starring role in one of my favorite stories. When one of his plays was about to open in London, Shaw sent a first-night ticket to Winston Churchill — two tickets, actually, inviting Churchill to attend and to "bring a friend, if you have one." Churchill sent back his thanks, saying he wouldn't be able to attend the opening, and added: "Will attend the second night, if there is one."

The Very First Coach?

Early in my coaching career I ran across the military teachings of the Chinese general Sun Tzu, referred to earlier, and his book, *The Art of War*. I realized immediately how much his practical thinking — four centuries before Christ — translated so readily into coaching. For example:

> The good fighters of old first put themselves beyond the possibility of defeat, and then waited for an opportunity of defeating the enemy.

And:

> The opportunity to secure ourselves against defeat lies in our own hands, but the opportunity of defeating the enemy is provided by the enemy himself.

A very simple philosophy: Find ways to let the other side beat itself.

P.S., Initials of Another Early Coach

Just a few hundred years after Sun Tzu came Publilius Syrus, a Roman who was the originator of wise sayings that have lived for 2,000-plus years. For example:

> A rolling stone gathers no moss.

As a coaching advisory, I liked this one even better:

> Pardon one offense and you encourage the commission of many.

Also:

> Nothing can be done at once hastily and prudently.
> Anyone can hold the helm when the sea is calm.
> There are some remedies worse than the disease.
> Practice is the best of all instructors.

The latter is better than "practice makes perfect," because that one presumes the practice itself was good. Practice is the best of all instructors, if the person running the practice knows what the hell he or she is doing. Improvement, especially toward perfection, comes only if the practice is demanding, well-thought-out, and constructive, by a coach who realizes that absolute perfection is unattainable — but is always the objective.

It isn't only in coaching that this one from Publilius Syrus works:

> I have often regretted my speech, never my silence.

That's a better way of saying "Go to shut-up school."
Of all, this one from Publilius may be my favorite:

> It is a bad plan that admits of no modification.

Every successful endeavor starts with a plan. Know that some things will go wrong. *Adjust* is one of the great words in the English language. Always, no matter how meticulously something has been thought out and planned, an effective leader has to be ready and willing to adjust.

I learned quickly in my early days as head coach at Army that the title of basketball coach didn't carry much clout at West Point. I would call an officer at the academy, and the noncom or corporal taking the call would ask, "Who's calling?" For a time, I said, "This is Bob Knight, the basketball coach," and invariably I would get back some version of "He's unavailable right now. Try again later."

Then one day I read that there were 450 active generals in the Army at that time, and I figured, "Eisenhower and MacArthur couldn't know all of them." I saw an active list, ran down it, and came up with one name that wasn't present. So I invented No. 451.

From then on, I'd make my calls, and when I got the identification question, I'd snap, "General Webster." And I'd hear, "Yes, sir!" and get right through.

Adjust is a vitally important word.

Speaking of Quotations . . .

What I've seen referred to as history's greatest speeches implore and inspire, many times negatively.

Perhaps America's greatest speech, certainly one of its favorites, was Lincoln's Gettysburg Address, which in just over 230 words included a number of negatives, yet is one of the greatest declarations of our positive principles of democratic government.

> But, in a larger sense, we can NOT dedicate—we can NOT consecrate—we can NOT hallow—this ground. The world will little note, nor long remember . . . these dead shall NOT have died in vain . . . government of the people, by the people, for the people, shall NOT perish from the earth.

Franklin D. Roosevelt's first inaugural address twice used a negative-image word to—memorably and historically—make his own positive point:

> The only thing we have to fear is fear itself.

John F. Kennedy's inaugural address is most remembered for:

> Ask NOT what your country can do for you—ask what you can do for your country.

Two of our most respected presidents, George Washington and Dwight Eisenhower, are not really remembered for speeches they made while in office, but they are revered today for their prophetic farewells. Most memorable in those farewells were not their hip-hip-hoorays or their optimism for the country but their cautions, their warnings of dangers to watch out for.

The Prescient "Father" President

George Washington's farewell address — not truly a speech but a 6,000-word document sent to Congress as his final days in office approached — is noted most for its warning against entangling international alliances, which was timely to a young nation then and has become even more relevant some 200 years later. With the benefit of Washington's foresight and our own hindsight, how do we now feel about Vietnam, Iraq, Afghanistan? His negative counsel about entangling foreign alliances stands as very positive advice for our nation today.

Washington also warned us about the whole concept of political parties. Again, he was more than 200 years ahead of the most recent Democrat-Republican congressional stalemates:

> The alternate domination of one faction over another, sharpened by the spirit of revenge, natural to party dissension . . . is itself a frightful despotism. . . . It serves always to distract the public councils and enfeeble the public administration. It agitates the community with ill-founded jealousies and false alarms, kindles the animosity of one part against another . . .

He saw those dangers to good government without even exposure to today's runaway election expenses. For the presidency alone, what is more wasteful than the multimillions of dollars raised and spent for presidential primaries? All evidence is that today, the true best and brightest of our potential national leaders have no appetite for entering into the long, long months of primaries, raising and spending those multi-millions, exhausting all that money and themselves, getting their careers dissected and maligned. Then, the "lucky" winner emerging in the fall is usually so smeared by his primary rivals that the other party simply has to raise a few reminders of what a candidate's own party "friends" had said about him or her. Hell of a system, after more than 230 years of the evolution of our democracy.

I have two suggestions that have no real chance of happening, but are worth considering. First, bring back the "smoke-filled rooms" to develop each party's candidates. Second, change the Constitution so that the President serves a six-year term without a possibility of re-election. That way the President doesn't have to spend the first four-year term worrying about re-election while the opposition party works at "enfeebling" the President, as Washington warned.

The Other General-President's Farewell Warnings

Then there was Dwight Eisenhower. In two-term Ike's farewell address in 1960, one of America's great war generals was the first to use the term "military-industrial complex" in warning against our civilian government's inability to control the powerful partnership of military and large corporations.

Crises there will continue to be . . . there is a recurring tempta-
tion to feel that some spectacular and costly action could become the miraculous solution to all current difficulties. . . . But
each proposal must be weighed in the light of a broader con-
sideration: the need to maintain balance in and among national programs . . . Our toil, resources and livelihood are all
involved; so is the very structure of our society. We must guard
against the acquisition of unwarranted influence, whether
sought or unsought, by the military-industrial complex. . . .
Only an alert and knowledgeable citizenry can compel the
proper meshing of the huge industrial and military machinery
of defense with our peaceful methods and goals.

Keep in mind: An army general said that. I would argue
that we should be proud of our military for the bravery of our
soldiers, but we should take a very negative view of wasting
our resources in meaningless wars that wind up costing bil-
lions of dollars and cause untold grief in the lives of our troops
and their families.

Words That Never Grow Old

The most beloved passage in our Declaration of Indepen-
dence says:

We hold these truths to be self-evident, that all men are cre-
ated equal, that they are endowed by their Creator with certain unalienable Rights, that among these are Life, Liberty and
the pursuit of Happiness.

And later says:

> ... whenever any Form of Government becomes destructive of these ends, it is the Right of the People to alter or to abolish it, and to institute new Government.

No tolerating the status quo there. No looking for the sun to come up tomorrow. If our system is broken, we need to fix it.

Time to change.

Shakespeare's most famous speech, maybe the most famous eulogy in all of literature, was Marc Antony's at Julius Caesar's funeral. It is classic satire, which brings into play negative after negative, right from his lead-in — "I come to bury Caesar, *not* to praise him" — and stirs up hatred for conspirators Brutus and Cassius with constant sarcastic references to them as "honorable men." This speech is also a statement of indignation at how easily we can lose our collective judgment and allow it to be undermined by "brutish beasts." Here is a true ode to skepticism and verification.

> *The evil that men do lives after them;*
> *The good is oft interred with their bones;*
> *So let it be with Caesar. The noble Brutus*
> *Hath told you Caesar was ambitious:*
> *If it were so, it was a grievous fault;*
> *And grievously hath Caesar answer'd it.*

Here, under leave of Brutus and the rest —
For Brutus is an honorable man;
So are they all, all honorable men —
Come I to speak in Caesar's funeral.
He was my friend, faithful and just to me:
But Brutus says he was ambitious;
And Brutus is an honorable man . . .

I speak not to disprove what Brutus spoke,
But here I am to speak what I do know.
You all did love him once, not without cause:
What cause withholds you, then, to mourn for him?
O judgment, thou art fled to brutish beasts,
And men have lost their reason. Bear with me;
My heart is in the coffin there with Caesar,
And I must pause till it come back to me.

Straight from the Bible, straight from the pages of history, straight from Shakespeare, the great messages, the great teachings, the great advisories, even the great leadership has frequently come from a "negative" or wary perspective. Yet, none was meant to offer a negative resolution. Quite the contrary. All aimed at building the fortitude of bullets dodged, of hurdles spotted in time, of hazards avoided, while resisting judgments clouded by false emotion or selfish yearnings.

It was Abraham Lincoln who took Antony's warning a little further when he said, "You can please some of the people all the time and all of the people some of the time, but you can't please all of the people all of the time." That was a brilliant projection of the inherent weakness in our society where politicians abandon their leadership responsibilities and try to curry favor, money, and votes by reading the polls and chaining themselves to their constituents' ever-changing desires.

Here is one final story to punctuate Lincoln's warning:

On the way to market, an old man and his young grandson meet a man going the other way. The stranger says, "Old man, you should have your grandson riding the mule." So he puts his grandson on the mule. They go a little farther, they're stopped again, and a different man says, "Boy, you should let your poor grandfather ride the mule while you guide it." So they switch, go a little farther, and they're stopped again by a man who tells them, "You should both be riding the mule," so both get on the mule and continue toward market. They meet a fourth man who tells them. "Hey, you two, it's not very kind of you to be riding and creating that much of a burden for your poor mule." So they get off, and they all go a little farther before a fifth man says, "You know, grandfather and grandson, that mule looks tired to me. You two ought to carry the mule." So grandfather and grandson pick up the mule and trudge along. As they're crossing a bridge over a river, the old man slips, they both lose their balance and fall, and they accidentally drop the mule over the bridge into the water, and it drowns.

Which I think just extends Lincoln's point: *If you try to please everybody, you're going to lose your ass.*

KNIGHT'S NUGGETS

These are filter cigarettes — they're safe, I hear.

And you'll meet the nicest people who smoke them in your cancer ward.

I can make it through that yellow light.

And the driver of that big truck coming on your left has the same idea about getting a jump on the green light.

This time of the year, the ice on that lake could hold up a car.

Age-old Indian proverb: When crossing icy pond, never go first.

5

Napoleon, Hitler, and Other Positivists

I N BASKETBALL, I BELIEVE the coach who gets caught up with envisioning good things, with "positive imaging," risks having the possibility of losing never even entering his mind. So he tends to overlook problems he needs to prepare for.

The coach who recognizes the possibility—maybe even in specific cases the probability—of losing is going to work a lot harder, and my favorite example comes out of my college major, history, not a basketball record book. It's the 1948 presidential election.

Harry Truman was the incumbent, a pretty much unknown Missouri senator when Franklin Roosevelt put him on his ticket in 1944, and the man who was thrust into Roosevelt's chair when the popular president died three months into his fourth term. The atomic bomb decision and final victory over both Germany and Japan came under Truman, but all the bloom was off that by 1948.

A country that had been so united in war was on the verge of splitting apart in peace, and that unrest took its toll on the popularity of the man who made his acceptance of responsibility famous with the sign on his desk that read THE BUCK STOPS HERE. Long before the '48 campaign's start, the media — newspapers, magazines, and radio in those days — made Thomas E. Dewey, the New York governor who had given even Roosevelt a strong run in 1944, the odds-on favorite to beat the unexciting incumbent Truman.

That was his dilemma even before Truman lost the left wing in his party when Henry Wallace, the ultra-liberal whom Roosevelt had dumped as vice president, put Truman on the ticket in '44, to lead a third national party called Progressives.

Then he lost the right wing in his party when support for desegregation, a rising cause in America, split the 1948 Democratic convention and a fourth ultra-conservative party was formed to oppose desegregation: the States' Rights Democratic Party or "Dixiecrats." Strom Thurmond headed the Dixiecrats, and its Deep South popularity threatened what had been the Democratic Party's dependable electoral-vote harvest from what it called the "Solid South."

Nobody thought poor, simple ol' Harry had a chance when the homestretch campaign began around Labor Day 1948. Truman was left in the situation that French marshal Ferdinand Foch, commander in chief of Allied forces in World War I, had recognized in one of history's most famous battleground messages:

My center is giving way,
My right is in retreat;
Situation excellent!
I shall attack!

Like Foch, who sent out that message and then stopped a German advance and turned World War I around at the Marne with his retreat-checking attack, Truman — his left and right departed — attacked: With strong, plain-speaking language usually delivered from the back of a railroad train, Truman blasted away at Dewey and what he called the "do-nothing [Republican-led] Congress." It was the last pretelevision election. Truman's spirited one-man campaign was aimed beyond the media, straight at voting Americans. Truman railed at the opposition while growing crowds urged him on, with the slogan "Give 'em hell, Harry!" — and he gave 'em plenty of that. Though polls to the end said he had no chance, Truman won in an unimaginable upset (the everlasting memorial to it being the *Chicago Tribune*'s famously inaccurate picture on page one, headlined "DEWEY DEFEATS TRUMAN").

First, both Dewey and Truman had to size up their situation, recognizing the futility of letting things just happen, and then they went to work. As the conventions ended and the campaign began, Truman had to know what the polls and newspapers and magazines all were saying and concluded: "He is right now in a better position to win than I am. I have to work a lot harder than he does, spend a lot more time and be a lot more effective with the public . . ."

If . . . then . . .

If I do this, *then* I have a chance. And *if* I don't . . .

And Dewey, filled with overconfidence, maneuvered his way into losing an election that seemed safely in his hands. All he had to do was play it safe, not rock the boat. He and his handlers had to be thinking of all the clichés that "sure" winners use on their way to defeat. In competitive situations, until the issue is decided, a sense of security is dangerous.

At least Dewey's mistake was bloodless. Military history is full of foolish mistakes by national leaders and battlefield commanders — based on misplaced optimism about how a risky move would assure victory. The human and financial cost is almost incalculable. All those missteps — all our modern-day wars with high-tech weapons against Sun Tzu practitioners that look so easy to the fat cats who make war decisions at no risk to themselves — these are the ultimate perils of positive thinking. Obviously, this is a consuming concern of mine, perhaps so personal for me because of all those great kids I worked with at West Point.

But I'm not alone. From talks I have given and responses I have seen, I can tell you there are mothers and dads, grandmas and grandpas out there whose love of country is not at all in question but who hate seeing kids come back victims of a national commitment they don't understand for a purpose they can't conceive. Somebody in Washington should understand there's a nation out there that doesn't see the worth of what all we're investing in these unending wars that began with such positive assurances.

The Pogo Principle

My favorite statement on perplexing dilemmas was made by the Walt Kelly cartoon character Pogo, who said: "We have met the enemy and he is us."

Pogo is on my board of directors of Negative Thinking, Inc., because you can read into that statement all kinds of things. I read: "we" haven't worked hard enough, "we" haven't prepared well enough, "we" haven't given enough thought to what we have to do to win, so "we" are absolutely the reason why we are getting beaten.

We *are* our own worst enemy when we are overconfident, when we don't pay attention to the small details, when we think we are going to win just because of who we are and what we *think* we are. If there is one lesson from international events these days, it's that we must always keep Pogo in mind. We are not the Goliath that we think we are, and that's why we're getting our ass kicked. Or, as the great football coach Vince Lombardi frequently put it from the sideline when his team was playing in subpar fashion: "What the hell is going *on* out there?" He was a tough realist who understood that things don't change on their own.

A Man Named Pyrrhus

Sometimes even victory isn't enough; hence the term "won the battle but lost the war." It even has a name: a *Pyrrhic victory.* Around 280 BC in Epirus, a tiny southeastern European nation that now would be between Albania and Greece, a courageous king named Pyrrhus led his army to a bloody but costly victory over the forces of the vast and mighty Roman Empire. Pyrrhus had no real choice; his greatly outmanned nation was attacked by the powerful Roman army. His victory was brilliantly planned and carried out, a spectacular triumph.

But he knew it was more a case of forestalling the inevitable than truly winning. His heavy manpower losses even in victory, and Rome's unending supply of troops to rush in as replacements (as opposed to his nation's skimpy population), left Pyrrhus shaking his head as he—according to history—said dryly amid congratulations, "One more such victory will undo me!" The idea of a Pyrrhic victory was born.

What Pyrrhus said in inspiring the term was basically neither negative nor positive thinking, just a wise analysis of his desperate situation—and showed why he was such an important leader that he is one of the subjects of Plutarch's *Lives*.

Another example of a costly victory was Pearl Harbor. There is a scene in the movie *Tora! Tora! Tora!* where Japanese admiral Isoroku Yamamoto holds his head amid celebration of his country's successful sneak attack and says, "I fear all we have done is to awaken a sleeping giant and fill him with a terrible resolve." (That statement has never been documented, but some say the remark does show up in his diary.)

True quotation or not, the surprise one-day attack was for the Empire of Japan a Pyrrhic victory: spectacular today, costly tomorrow. (Now, as movie lines go, I much prefer the one in the 1970 movie *Patton*, with General George Patton in front of an American flag and telling his troops, "I want you to remember that no bastard ever won a war by dying for his country. He won it by making the other poor dumb bastard die for his country.") Tragically, not nearly enough generals understood that, and men died—on both sides in every war—for the sake of dumb military decisions.

Nothing illustrates that more vividly than two historic examples: Napoleon and Hitler attacking Russia.

Bad coaching.

Napoleon had seemed invincible until he invaded Russia with 500,000 men and returned with 27,000 in a six-month venture in 1812 that decimated his army, shattered his reputation, and ended his European conquests. That total miscalculation did give the world two classics: Tolstoy's *War and Peace* (ancient rule: History is written by the winners) and Tchaikovsky's *1812 Overture* (so joyfully triumphant and played so often at Fourth of July festivals that most of America must think it celebrates *our* War of 1812).

Hitler must not have read Tolstoy, though his advisors did. Invade *Russia?* Don't even *think* about doing it, they said. What is there about *"Those who cannot remember the past are condemned to repeat it"* that you don't understand, Adolf? Much, apparently. Ego drove him to do what Napoleon couldn't do, probably *because* Napoleon couldn't. We can only be grateful. Some negative thinking on Hitler's part probably wouldn't have changed the ultimate outcome of the war, but it surely would have pushed back V-E Day in America and cost us additional lives.

Both Napoleon and Hitler thought their armies were far superior to Russia's and it wouldn't be much of a chore to subdue the Russians. Yet neither really *looked* at the competition — neither *understood* the playing field, the vast number of soldiers that the Russians could put on the field, the desire, the backs-to-the-wall determination of the Russian people because of their love for their homeland.

And they were blindest of all to the sheer logistics — how savage the Russian winter was, how far their troops had to go to fight, and how far they had to return. Hitler had been so confident of quick victory — victory before winter came — that his troops' uniforms were much too light for temperatures that reached 20 degrees below zero. His tanks were inoperative in the Russian winter mud. Napoleon's manpower loss was a fraction of Hitler's (and Russia's), but each left there doomed — because of blind optimism, because of the peril of positive thinking without really *thinking things through.*

On the other hand, before Napoleon, in the harsh winter of 1776, American general George Washington avoided a potential death blow to his troops on Long Island, held them back from conflict, and attacked later in the tide-turning battle of Trenton. And thus he lived to see America become a nation.

Bravado leads to far more failure than does caution. At Gettysburg, Confederate general Robert E. Lee's overzealous ambition led to Major General George Pickett's reckless third-day charge, in which his troops were annihilated by Union forces. It doesn't take a military genius to stand near the battlefields at Gettysburg and see how foolhardy was that historic charge that never should have been attempted — the odds were too great. A more cautious negative thinker would have attacked by going around the Union army or, smarter yet, left altogether to fight on a different day. Confederate general James Longstreet, in fact, pleaded with Lee to leave the battlefield after the second day. Had he listened . . .

I felt after my first visit to the hallowed battlefield that Lee's sending Pickett's soldiers across more than 500 yards of open field, charging along Yankee lines of fire, is enough in itself to eliminate him from any list of great American generals. A book just out, written by a professional military historian, substantiates my instincts and cites as the preeminent authority the Chinese military genius Sun Tzu. In fact, the book's title is *Sun Tzu at Gettysburg,* and the author, Bevan Alexander, says:

> The battle of Gettysburg provides enlightening instruction on how generals estimate terrain and evaluate the dispositions of the enemy. What they *see* varies enormously among individuals. An observant person looking at the landscape of Gettysburg is struck almost at once by the dominance of Round Top at the southern end of the ridgeline. The hill soars above the other terrain features. For a person with imagination — most especially for a seasoned military officer who should have special knowledge about enfilade fire — it stands forth as the true place for cannons. But quite clearly Lee did not see it or ignored it. . . .

Sun Tzu might have been speaking of a situation similar to what happened on Gettysburg's climactic day, July 3, when he said, "One who knows when he *can* fight, and when he *cannot* fight, will be victorious." Sun Tzu emphasizes that "there is terrain for which one does not contend." There is no better example of such terrain than the strong Union positions running from Cemetery Hill and Culp's Hill, along Cemetery Ridge, and anchored at Little Round Top on July 3. Lee should have realized that a frontal attack targeting the center of the Union line on Cemetery Ridge — "terrain for which one does not contend" — was an action that his army "cannot fight."

Another outstanding basketball coach who preceded and befriended me — Stu Inman — was the person who introduced me to the insights into good coaching that Sun Tzu's theories convey, even if he was writing in 400 BC.

One of his cardinal rules of war was avoiding head-on confrontations, always preferring to probe for weaknesses, for points of vulnerability, rather than attempting to overpower the enemy. This is my favorite Sun Tzu-ism, and one directly applicable to basketball planning:

Water shapes its course according to the nature of the ground over which it flows; the soldier works out his victory in relation to the foe whom he is facing.

Therefore, just as water retains no constant shape, so in warfare there are no constant conditions.

He who can modify his tactics in relation to his opponent and thereby succeed in winning may be called a heaven-born captain.

I can't imagine any leader who would find a compliment better than being called "a heaven-born captain."

West Point, which produced all the major Civil War leaders on both sides, cannot be faulted for failure to teach Sun Tzu's theories. Even in textbook form, those were unknown by Western military decision-makers throughout history up until World War II. Though dating to shortly after the time of Alexander the Great, Sun Tzu's principles weren't translated into the English book *The Art of War* until years after they had surfaced within China, and that was more than 2,000 years after they were written. Mao Tse-tung was the first modern military leader to happen on them, and he incorporated them into his own textbook for the guerrilla warfare technique with which he ultimately took over China. They surfaced again in Vietnam and everywhere else where outmanned local forces have withstood vastly more powerful outside forces.

It was in Mao's guerrilla days in 1936 that he wrote, Sun

Tzu–style, "Ingenious devices such as making a noise in the east and attacking in the west, appearing now in the south and now in the north, hit-and-run and night action should be constantly employed to mislead, entice, and confuse the enemy." In football, it's called misdirection; in basketball, cat-and-mouse, but to my mind there are all too many Lees coaching out there, not just in football, convinced that it's somehow unmanly or unworthy to win any way but by matching power with power.

The one Confederate general who practiced Sun Tzu's principles was Stonewall Jackson, of whom Alexander wrote: "If there ever was an intellectual descendant of Sun Tzu, it was Stonewall Jackson. His methods in the campaigns of 1862 embodied virtually all of Sun Tzu's primary axioms: avoid strength, strike at weakness, go around the enemy, use deception not power to overcome, seize something the enemy must seek to recover, and induce the enemy to attack well-prepared positions and be defeated." But, time and again, Jackson's suggestions were rejected or ignored by the confrontation-minded Lee. By Gettysburg, Jackson was unavailable even to argue, killed weeks earlier at Chancellorsville.

Alexander contends that if Lee had given Jackson the 5,000 men he requested for a daring, guerrilla-style invasion of the north, all history might have been changed.

Jackson . . . sought to strike at the heart of Union power, its factories, cities, and railroads. This embodies Sun Tzu's most profound advice: to destroy the very will of the enemy to resist. A drive into the North could have won the war for the South in weeks. But Jackson was unable to induce the Confederate president, Jefferson Davis, and his military adviser, Robert E. Lee, to carry out this campaign. Davis and Lee abandoned Jackson's war of maneuver and took up a long war of attrition, of slowly wearing down resistance. This was a war that the South, with one-eleventh of the industry and one-third of the manpower of the North, was bound to lose. . . . when Davis and Lee refused the admonitions of Jackson, the destiny of the United States of America was determined.

Pickett, whose name — not Lee's — is attached to the blunder that marked Gettysburg, survived the "charge" that half his 12,000-man unit didn't. He came out of it more of a realist than some positive-thinking, losing coaches do. He's credited with, years later, answering a question about what went wrong that day: "I've always thought the Yankees had something to do with it."

Pickett Had a Predecessor

Among the blessings of my Orrville childhood was that electronic games hadn't been invented yet. When I wasn't playing some kind of ball, I spent a lot of time at the town library, and

I pretty much went through the full stock of my school library as well, particularly biographies. The only card game of the day I remember was Authors, which involved trying to get full sets of works by some of the greatest writers through history. One of them was Tennyson, and one of his three book cards — really, a poem — was "Charge of the Light Brigade."

When I read the poem on the card, it became more than a playing card to me. I realized it wasn't at all an epic work praising the military heroism of courageous soldiers, but Alfred, Lord Tennyson's immediate recognition — as England's poet laureate — of his nation's terrible military blunder at Balaclava on October 25, 1854, in the Crimean War against Russia. Pickett's Charge at Gettysburg came about a decade later. Indeed, Bevan Alexander in *Sun Tzu at Gettysburg* says, "Pickett's Charge should be seen as a vastly magnified version of the Charge of the Light Brigade at Balaclava in the Crimean War — as an act of lunacy or perversity by a commander who ignored better counsel and brought on a disaster that could and should have been avoided."

Both involved an ordered charge on an impossible mission — Tennyson's by an elite cavalry group, the 600-man Light Brigade. Tennyson, within hours of hearing details of Balaclava, gave England's blunder some of the most memorable phrases in all war literature:

Half a league, half a league,
*   Half a league onward,*
All in the Valley of Death
*   Rode the six hundred.*
"Forward, the Light Brigade!
*   "Charge for the guns!" he said:*
Into the Valley of Death
*   Rode the six hundred.*

"Forward, the Light Brigade!"
*   Was there a man dismay'd?*
Not tho' the soldier knew
*   Someone had blundered:*
Theirs not to make reply,
Theirs but to do and die:
Into the Valley of Death
Rode the six hundred.
Cannon to right of them,
*   Cannon to left of them,*
Cannon in front of them
*   Volley'd and thunder'd;*
Storm'd at with shot and shell,
Boldly they rode and well,
Into the jaws of Death,

Into the mouth of Hell
  Rode the six hundred.

. . .

When can their glory fade?
O the wild charge they made!
All the world wondered.
Honor the charge they made,
Honor the Light Brigade,
  Noble six hundred.

"Half a league, half a league, half a league onward" . . . "Theirs not to reason why, theirs but to do and die" . . . "Into the valley of Death rode the six hundred" . . . "Cannon to right of them, cannon to left of them, Cannon in front of them, Volley'd and thunder'd" . . . "Not tho' the soldier knew, Someone had blunder'd."

Six segments of it, seventeen of its fifty-five lines, are in Bartlett's *Familiar Quotations* — classic, unforgettable phrasing — a monument to courage, yes, but also to leadership stupidity. Reading history from the Spartans and Greeks through World War I, I have constantly been amazed by the number of frontal attacks — an entrenched enemy simply firing at the attackers as they crossed open fields, as they rode or charged or marched straight into a "valley of death."

Rely *on* You

Sometimes things I read just stick in my mind, and I can't really cite where I saw them.

Lincoln said an important thing for any leader to understand is: Do what *you* think is best — after, I'm presuming, you've thoroughly thought out and researched the problem. I'd like to think even Abe, with his profound faith, made his judgments on something more than divine guidance.

Someone of considerably less stature than Lincoln had advice almost as profound: Don't start vast projects with half-vast ideas.

I'm sure you'll never find that in Bartlett's, but I like it — and it starts with *don't*.

Here's an optimist story I did appreciate. A pessimism-inclined young boy who had been dreaming of getting a pony for Christmas raced out to the family barn that morning and — in the place where he had been told his Christmas gift was — found nothing but piles of horse manure. He slammed the barn door behind him and went back to the house, sobbing.

Down the road, the same thing happened to his optimistic buddy. When he opened the barn door and saw the same thing, he let out a gleeful howl and dashed into the middle of the stench, shouting, "Where there's this much horse shit, somewhere there's gotta be a pony!"

And a not-so-fast negativist I liked even better:

Two bulls, one young and one old, looked down from a hilltop onto a meadow full of prancing young cows. The young bull snorted and said, "Out of my way, old man. I'm gonna run right down there and service me one."

And the old bull answered: "Patience, son. Walk down and service them all."

6

Negative Thinking in the First Job

WHEN I GRADUATED from Ohio State, I wasn't yet twenty-two, but I knew what I wanted to be in life: a basketball coach. I had some thoughts about going to law school — my dad, who never could see coaching as anything close to a profession or even a reliable way to make a living, certainly would have preferred that. But I came out of Ohio State knowing that I truly wanted to coach, and right away, I had the opportunity to become a head coach at a couple of different Ohio high schools.

I was as eager to get going as any other kid coming out of college into the job market. The offers were there because the whole state of Ohio knew about the guys who had been part of the great Ohio State basketball era Fred Taylor had launched —

three straight Big Ten championships (1960–62), three straight trips to the national championship game, one NCAA championship. Other guys in my senior class were the headliners: College Player of the Year Jerry Lucas, the guy I still consider the best Big Ten player ever; John Havlicek, my all-time favorite basketball player; All-Big Ten guard Mel Nowell, a three-year starter—*great* hands, great quickness. From our class, those were the "names" on those championship teams. But all our names were known throughout Ohio.

In the weeks after our last college season we seniors—Lucas, Havlicek, Nowell, Gary Gearhart, and I—went around the state barnstorming against local teams and made a lot of money for ourselves. Lucas, Havlicek, and Nowell drew the people in, but I was one from our group not going to the pros, *the* one who wanted to coach. So I was in a good position to be hired.

With no experience at all, I interviewed for the head coaching job at a well-regarded Ohio high school. I felt it could have been a great place to start right out, and I had reason to believe I could have had the job if I wanted it.

I had all the ego-inflating reasons why a young man in that position normally would consider himself ready to grab such an opportunity. I had played the game from sixth grade through four years of college under some outstanding coaches. And I had played for a very poor coach, which taught me something else that was very important: what *not* to do. Overall, I made a list of what I liked and what I didn't like from all those coaches and used it as a guideline for how I intended to coach.

The decision I made right there was my first professional acknowledgment of *The Power of Negative Thinking*.

Eager as I might have been, I simply didn't think I knew *how* to *coach*. So I passed on pursuing a head coaching job to become an assistant coach under a veteran and highly respected coach: Harold "Andy" Andreas, at Cuyahoga Falls High School just outside Akron.

Fifty years and a whole lifetime in coaching later, I consider that the second most important career decision I ever made. I had learned a lot about *playing* basketball from the excellent coaches I'd had, but my real education in coaching and teaching the game started with Andy.

One of the first things he taught me was to understand what my players could do, and — even more important — what they could not do, relative to the skills of the game. He was a great believer in not overloading his players with so much information that they weren't able to react instinctively to what was happening on the floor.

As a would-be coach, I didn't feel I could get enough information from him. I spent all the time I could that season asking him questions. My job included scouting for the varsity team as well as coaching the junior varsity team. When I'd give Andy my scouting report on an upcoming opponent, he would question me about everything, every *aspect* of everything that opponent did — each individual player, the team, every scrap of information he could get from me. Very quickly I learned to scout better, so I wouldn't be embarrassed by my inability to answer the questions, but I also learned about coaching — that it was imperative to be well prepared, with an approach to each individual game that gave your team its best chance to win.

I took from this experience that you could never dare to feel in good shape to win just because your players were better than the other team's — even if they were. I learned that you can't come away from a really good performance feeling that your team would automatically play well in the next game. And that was true even quarter to quarter in the same game.

Same Game, Different View

Andy was the source of what became one of my strongest coaching beliefs: that mistakes determine the outcome of far more games than great plays do. Until then, I was a player who thought we could go out on a basketball court and make the plays that would just beat an opponent. He and his assistant, Bill Raybuck, taught me I was right, but not about *how* we would win. We'd do it by doing what *we* do better than we let them do what *they* do.

One of our junior varsity games was against Barberton as a preliminary to the schools' varsity game. Their JV team came into the game undefeated. I went to Andy with a plan I had worked out: to use a half-court trapping zone press as our defense. He listened to me, and then said, "If you can't figure out how to beat a team with our man-to-man defense, you are never going to be a good coach." I got the hint. We played them man-to-man and won.

There was a philosophy behind what he was saying. Pete Newell, the great coach of college championship teams at San Francisco (NIT, 1949) and California (NCAA, 1959) and the gold-medal 1960 U.S. Olympic team, became in my later coaching years what Harold Andreas was in my earliest: a friend and invaluable advisor. Pete once told me, unknowingly reinforcing what Andy had done with that defensive insistence, that there were two kinds of coaches: those who favored surprise and change, and those who favored simplicity and execution — and the surprise-and-change teams were never drilled to be as effective in their play as the simplicity-and-execution teams were.

Oh, Pete knew the surprise-and-change guys always impressed the media and fans with the number of offenses and defenses they would use in a game. But simplicity-and-execution teams — Vince Lombardi's Green Bay Packers were a supreme example — were taught to do the things they could do best, which minimizes mistakes.

Before Lombardi there was Paul Brown, a boyhood idol of mine as a devout Cleveland Browns fan. Lombardi and Brown brought about the whole concept of eliminating mistakes. I coached basketball, they coached football, but I styled a lot of my basic thinking along their ways — and the ways of other fundamentalists in basketball, high up among the Hall of Famers on that list being Pete Newell, as well as Henry Iba, Clair Bee, Joe Lapchick, Everett Dean, my own Ohio State coach, Fred Taylor — I never hesitated to ask *any* of them questions.

One of the greatest compliments I ever received in coaching was a short note from Dave Gavitt, the Providence College and U.S. Olympic coach who called me "the greatest teacher in coaching today." That comment, from the man whom I consider the father of the Big East basketball conference, was one I treasured because I always felt my primary role *was* as a teacher — a demanding teacher!

The key to consistent execution is to be demanding. The word *demand* is important in leadership success. *Demand* is a negative word, since it assumes a critical lack of action or production. The best teachers and the best leaders are the most demanding people I've known — intelligently demanding. Don't demand of people what they can't do. Demand what they can do.

Always remember that the people you lead are going to be satisfied with the minimum of what you demand. Maximum results come from maximum expectations — not unrealistic, but maximum. Tolerant people do not make good leaders. Successful leadership is being hard to please — and your players or employees or students know it. They will settle for what you tolerate. A great leader is an intolerant one.

I always wanted to bring out in my players, too, that quality of being able to demand excellence among themselves. Starting with the first teams I coached at West Point, my teams never elected captains. *I* picked the captains, players I thought had played hard or I knew I could count on the most, and I'd tell them, "It isn't just you playing hard. It's you making other guys play hard. I can't do it all. *You've* got to demand to other guys that *they* have to play harder. You've got to get *on* these guys."

I always told parents of recruits that I would be the most demanding coach their son would ever play for, and it would carry over into all phases of life: his academic work, his career, his conduct as a family man. I wanted to make sure he and his parents understood that before he ever got started playing for me.

Recruiting was where demands had to start. I was often asked what was most critical to me in evaluating potential recruits. It's a good question, but not one that fits into any formula.

First of all, I wanted players who were going to be the most difficult to play against, because of their athletic ability and the way I thought they could play defensively, learning and accepting my mistake-avoidance strategy. Then I thought about unselfishness. I also thought about skills. These kids were all good athletes, so their attitude was more important to me.

That didn't just pertain to recruiting. That's also how I put together two teams that won international gold medals. There, and in recruiting for my college teams, if I thought this was a kid used to doing everything his own way, I probably wasn't interested. There were times in recruiting when I just walked out of the house and said, "You know, I think you need to play someplace else." Maybe it was the kid's attitude toward his parents. I always judged recruits on general character.

Sometimes, even after you've decided to go after a player and you get him, you realize you want that player to be better than *he* wants to be. That's basically a kid who isn't going to work hard enough to get the most out of his talents, and in all probability is a kid you're wasting your time with. Spotting it in advance and avoiding that kind of situation is in the best interests of both the coach and the player — the employer and the employee.

West Point: My Biggest Break in Coaching

One of the satisfying things about my start in coaching under Andy Andreas at Cuyahoga Falls High School was that, after his own career in education had ended with retirement, I was able to bring him to Bloomington for something of a payback: He joined me as an assistant coach — a valued, contributing coach — just in time to go with me on the greatest ride a coach could have: our undefeated national-championship season at Indiana in 1976.

There was one vital step for me between Cuyahoga Falls and Bloomington.

At the end of my first season with Andy, I faced the last crucial decision: graduate school, maybe law school, or a continuation in coaching? Now I was twenty-two, and there was still an army draft — no real Vietnam threat yet, but the possibility of a draft. I exasperated my dad by volunteering to go into the army for two years, but I did it with a plan.

At the 1963 NCAA Final Four at Freedom Hall in Louisville just before the championship game between Loyola and Cincinnati, I was talking with Coach Taylor about what I wanted to do next: Go back to Cuyahoga Falls in a higher coaching position? Enter graduate school and do some coaching there? The coach at Army, George Hunter, was a friend of Coach Taylor, and he happened to hear our conversation. He told Coach Taylor, "If he's ever going to be drafted, let me know and I'll bring him to West Point." That wasn't really likely to happen, given the state of the draft then, but I said directly to Coach Hunter, "What would happen if I volunteer for the draft?" He said, "I'll bring you to West Point and you'll coach our plebe [freshman] team." (Fifty years later, I consider that question — "What would happen if I volunteered for the draft?" — the second-most important one I have ever asked in my life, only behind when I asked my future wife, Karen, to marry me.)

After that conversation with Coach Hunter, when I was off by myself with time to do some thinking, I did a little calculating. I had made $5,050 in my first year at Cuyahoga Falls: $4,600 for teaching four classes and a study hall, $450 for coaching. Bill Raybuck, who was Andy's assistant and an excellent coach, left to take a head coaching job, so I was going to be the varsity assistant, which meant more coaching money.

With that and an across-the-board salary increase for all teachers, my salary was going to jump 25 percent to about $6,300. And in addition, I had a chance to make $50 a game playing with some Cleveland Browns on a basketball team that in their off-season went around northern Ohio playing

THE POWER OF NEGATIVE THINKING

local teams—maybe as many as fifty games, so I was looking at another $2,500 on top of $6,300. For a kid who didn't have any obligations, that was pretty good—about $165 a week, average.

Wow!

All the reasons that would normally influence a young man's decision—starting with net income—were weighted against the choice I made. But I really didn't waver. I went into the army with a two-year commitment to stay in and serve. Everybody thought I was nuts, particularly my dad. But I told him, "If this works out, it's the best thing I could do in coaching. It's my second year out of college, and I'll already be involved in college coaching."

Then George Hunter got fired, and I was a little bit shaken. I had already volunteered, signed papers, and had a date to report. Maybe I could have gotten out of it, but I don't know. Coach Taylor called Coach Hunter, and Hunter assured him things were still all set for me with the new Army coach, Hunter's former assistant, Tates Locke.

When I got to West Point, I found out that wasn't quite the case—there were two or three other guys floating around in the army who had been told the same thing. But Tates, who was also young, just a couple of years older than me, had played at Ohio Wesleyan while I had been at Ohio State. So he knew where I was coming from, and that I had been with

Coach Taylor, so it worked out fine for me. I got the job and those other guys were left out there in the army. I was always really grateful that Tates had an Ohio background like mine, because I'm sure that influenced his taking me over those other guys.

So it was the best professional move that I ever made, even if it involved patience — a trait that has never been my strong suit. Everything started with ten weeks of basic training under the scorching summer sun at Fort Leonard Wood, Missouri — when my Orrville and college buddies were back home enjoying themselves. I won't deny that there were some days then when I even second-guessed myself. But I never questioned my choice in the way that most people judge jobs, by the bottom line. Strictly by the dollar, I had made a dumb move. The most I ever got for the next two years was $98 a month. West Point housed its nonrevenue sports opponents' players in an athletic dormitory, with room for enlisted coaches like me from the various academy sports. I lived there with three other guys: one coaching in lacrosse, one in soccer, and one as a trainer.

In those two years with Tates as the head coach and me as an assistant, we won forty games and lost fifteen. As my two-year commitment was ending, I had opportunities to go places as an assistant coach: to Cincinnati or the Naval Academy. He had offers, too, but I told Tates that he had to stay one more year and I would, too. We were again going to be very good that next year, which meant he was going to have three straight really good years on his résumé and be in position to get a great job.

He made what I considered a big mistake and left to go to Miami of Ohio — not even as the head coach but as the chief assistant, promised the head job later (which he got). That left me with the head coaching job at Army, as it turned out. But I'm convinced that only the athletic director who made that decision, Colonel Ray Murphy, hired me at twenty-four with no head coaching experience. He did it because he felt it was the right thing for Army basketball.

Suddenly, I was a head coach! And for my first two months as head coach, I was serving out my two-year commitment, still a Pfc., and still making $98 a month — thanks to Colonel Murphy, whom I kidded a lot because he was cheap. But he was a stickler: I had gone to Army on June 11, 1964; I was named head coach April 1, 1966; I got out of the Army June 10, 1966 — and *then* my salary became $6,500, with a place to live.

I had done exactly the right thing. If I hadn't made the choice I did, who knows what direction my career would have taken, how things would have wound up for me? I took a chance.

I learned an awful lot about college coaching at West Point. It isn't easy to recruit an athlete into any of the service academies, because of the post-graduation military commitment that each cadet faces — the very nature of what the army is all about makes West Point the most difficult of all on this score. But because it was so difficult to recruit there, it helped me with recruiting in the future.

Tates worked hard and believed in the equalizing power of a great defense. There's a Power of Negative Thinking principle involved in that realization alone: In coaching, you have to think negatively to *think* defense over offense, because you're saying — maybe even admitting — "We can't count on outscoring them; we have to figure out a way to stop *them*."

Advice from a Man Called Bud

Tates was another man who — like Andy Andreas — showed me how good preparation is vital to winning. And that covers defense, offense, and all phases that go into each. The success Tates's Army teams had and what followed in my six years there were the biggest testimonials I can cite to that credo that meant most to me: *Having the will to win is not enough. What matters is having the will to prepare to win.*

There's a story behind that philosophy. Late in my career, after the twenty-first century had begun and I had left Indiana, I spoke at the National Press Club in Washington, and Supreme Court Justice Clarence Thomas attended. We had talked before, and he told me that he carried in his billfold a newspaper clipping that attributed that quote to me. He was a big believer in that philosophy and complimented me for it. I appreciated that. I told him my thoughts along those lines stemmed from a conversation I had with former Oklahoma football coach Bud Wilkinson, although the actual phrasing was mine.

Bud was one of the great coaches in college football history — in *coaching* history, whatever the game. His teams at Oklahoma from 1953 to 1957 won *forty-seven* consecutive games. Think about that: During this streak there was a total turnover in personnel. The players who won the last dozen games were completely different from the guys who won the first dozen. That, I think, is the mark of a truly great coach. Must be, too, because no other team in more than 140 years of college football has won even forty straight.

Long after Bud had retired from coaching, I got to know him and visited with him several times. During one particular session, he told me two things that became absolute tenets of my approach to coaching. The first was: As the season moved past the halfway mark in games played, he'd meet with his coaches and ask each coach to write down the amount of time that should be spent in practice that afternoon. Then he invariably took the lowest number of minutes suggested. The highest might have been two-and-a-half hours, the lowest an hour and forty minutes. They'd go 1:40.

Here was negative thinking at work: Our players' legs are tired. We have to practice and practice hard, but we can't go as long as we have for two or three months now. Again, that word *can't*—here, as so many times when it's the key word and the right word, shorthand for counterproductive. What was being rejected—more practice time—would have hurt more than it helped.

From then on, I shortened practice with our teams as the year went on. That wasn't easy, because the final weeks of a season are the time when the most is on the line—the schedule is down to when a game or two can determine a championship—and it goes against instinct to cut back on work rather than go at it harder. But it's absolutely essential. Tired players don't think or play nearly as well as rested players. The great Vince Lombardi quote along those lines was "Fatigue makes cowards of us all."

As a result of that talk with Bud Wilkinson, after Christmas break I always set a limit of an hour and twenty minutes on a practice while other teams I knew were practicing three, three-and-a-half, even four hours. I think that one simple choice won us a lot of key late-season games, because in the last ten minutes we had fresher legs; we had not worn our kids down to the point where they couldn't play forty minutes of basketball at the pace the game requires. Their brains benefited, too. Not many good decisions are made by tired minds, in any walk of life.

Negative thinking — "We can't practice long at this time of the season" — didn't produce forty-seven straight wins for us as it did for Bud Wilkinson, but our Indiana teams in the '70s did win thirty-four in a row once and thirty-three another time, the two longest streaks in the history of the intensely competitive Big Ten.

A Key to Upsets

The second thing Bud Wilkinson talked to me about that day was the importance of preparation — how having a team well prepared going into a game was the most important thing a coach could do.

It was a great equalizer when the talent edge was on the other side. A great many of what the world calls "upsets" involve a very well-prepared lesser team beating a more talented team that wasn't.

How hard you've worked at preparation gives you the will to win. If you've prepared properly, you have the extra motivation to get a satisfactory return on your own investment of work, sweat, and focus.

I tell the story about the good athlete who had just graduated from college and had a very inquisitive mind. Before accepting one of the many attractive offers he had before him to go into business, he decided to make a trip around the world to see what it was all about. In South Africa, he was hired on as a guide on an expedition into the wilderness areas. He was excited — he was going to see a part of the world and the animal world that he had never seen.

The first day, as the youngest member of the party, he was bringing up the rear and carrying a forty-pound pack. Through the wilderness he walked and struggled, dropping a little behind the rest of the group. He rounded a bend, looked up, and saw on a rock dead ahead a full-grown lion crouched and ready to pounce — on him. The lion leaped! The young man's athletic skills kicked in: He dove just in time to get under the flying lion and escaped.

As the lion ran off, the unnerved young man pulled himself together and caught up with the rest of the group. That night, he slipped away from everyone else to reenter the jungle. This time he took his rifle with him to be a *lot* better prepared if that lion came around again. Away from the campsite, he practiced what he would do with his rifle and his new vigilance: He aimed his rifle at a bush, then at a tree limb, then picked out a target and fired — simulating an attack, preparing himself to be a better guide. He was starting to feel comfortable in his intense preparation when he came around a bend, and . . .

Up high, straight in front of him, was the same lion! Practicing shorter jumps.

> Moral: Even the will to prepare to win doesn't mean your opponent isn't preparing, too. And if he is and you aren't, the advantage is his.

Preparation Is Teaching

Everything that happened with the great young guys we had at Army reinforced that priority in my mind: preparation, preparation, preparation. There and everyplace else I coached, I knew teaching how to win was a big part of my job, and obviously it was all the more important in the development of a future officer. More than forty years after my Army days, a man I respect enormously as an observer of basketball, Five-Star Camp originator Howard Garfinkel, said my stay at West Point was the greatest coaching job in history because of the caliber of teams we played and frequently beat.

It was as high a compliment as I ever received, but it also had to cover the coachability of those West Point kids, who bought fully into the Power of Negative Thinking that was at the base of everything I taught: Our players bought into being hard to score against, which made us less fun to play against and much more difficult to defeat. Our bywords there, which stayed with me always:

> Winning with talent isn't necessarily the way to go about things.

> There are some things you can do and some things you can't do.

> Elimination of mistakes is more important than the will to win.

> Never let the status of the team we're playing affect the way we play.

To be good over any length of time is a constant drain on the leader. You have to keep your team at a high level, always. Don't let up. Don't deviate.

Negative thinking, the kind that helped me so much at the beginning of my career, would have been much wiser for me in my later career as well. My first sixteen years at Indiana University were under one president, John Ryan. During the later years of my twenty-nine-year stay there, I felt more and more that the administration and I were not on the same page, not marching to the same drum.

We were still winning a lot of games, still getting some great kids. I was still able to pay back to the university in ways that meant most to me — graduating our players, bringing major financial support to the university library. My positive thinking about what we had done and would continue to do convinced me that everything would go on as is for as long as I liked.

Negative thinking would have taken off the blinders and opened my eyes to what some good friends and wise counselors — Pete Newell, TV sportscaster Curt Gowdy, even coaching rival Al McGuire — were trying to tell me. I needed to say to myself, *I don't like these present administration people and can't and won't get along with them. . . . This is not going to get better — in fact almost certainly will deteriorate.* I was comfortable there, and comfort is a dangerous thing. Thinking positively about your future — blindly positively, without considering changes in circumstances — can be a real mistake.

Four years after I had gone to Texas Tech, similar things happened. We had built up to a position of some success, again with some great kids and outstanding administration support. Feeling very positive about the direction we were going, I turned down an offer to be the coach at the University of Tennessee. That was my second-biggest mistake. I should have thought about what I was doing, about the huge difference between those two places in a basketball sense — Texas Tech and Tennessee, Lubbock and Knoxville. I got wrapped up in how much I thought I owed Texas Tech when in reality I had more than paid that debt.

Lubbock is a hard place to recruit players to, because basketball is not vitally important to the people there. I talk about adages a lot. One of them is "the grass is always greener on the other side of the fence" — don't be too quick to jump. But the corollary is don't be blind to how thin the grass on your side of the fence might be getting. Don't be blind to negatives. Never allow what you consider positive things to override your ability to determine what the negatives of a situation are. Those negatives will always turn out to be more important than what feels "right" about a job. You can fool yourself about what is right.

I was very good about how I handled leaving West Point. I had chances to leave every one of my six years there. A lot of things were involved when I was in that job, including my appreciation for the opportunity I was given there when I had no credentials at all as a head coach. And I loved coaching there — enjoyed the challenge of working with the great kids that an academy gets. I knew that eventually I would have to leave, but I waited until it was just the right set of circumstances, the exact right place to go, and that's what Indiana was when I went there. There's no question: It was a great place for me, the absolute right place, for a long, long time.

Lubbock had some big pluses for me, particularly the people I met there. One of the best was probably the greatest football player the school ever turned out — E. J. Holub, a Lubbock kid who was an All-American and College Football Hall of Fame player at Tech, who then did something still unequaled in the Super Bowl: He started at linebacker for Kansas City in Super Bowl I and on the other side of the ball, as center, on the Chiefs team that beat Minnesota in Super Bowl IV.

E. J. was my Texas language coach, and he taught me a word that would have saved me a lot of syllables if I had heard it earlier: *sumbitch.* The first time we met, we were going across campus. He pointed out a guy and said, "Watch out for him. He's a bad sumbitch." Not long later, he introduced me to a guy and afterward said, "Now, that's a good sumbitch." I said, "Wait a minute — how can there be a good sumbitch and a bad one?" He just laughed, and he was as good a friend for me in my Lubbock years as he was a language teacher.

But for all the good people I met and grew to like in Lubbock, it was 180 degrees opposite from Bloomington in its love, its appreciation of basketball. An example that proved that most clearly to me came during the period when I was in the spotlight because we were about to win the game that — numerically — gave me the Division I men's coaching record for career wins.

Whatever I say about Lubbock's basic disinterest in basketball, that wasn't evident over the Christmas break in 2006. We weren't into the conference season yet; the big teams around the country were in a kind of holiday lull, so the college basketball spotlight was on something that had nothing to do with the polls or the "road to the Final Four" — the fact that, after about forty years with great players and great teams, I was within one of the career victory record of 879 Dean Smith had set over a similar period with great players and great teams at North Carolina.

We played Bucknell in a home game. Very good team — *mid-major* being the media term for the level at which they were consistently one of the best. They were the Butler of their day; they had beaten Kansas and Arkansas in successive years in the NCAA tournament. ESPN had guaranteed them a nationally televised game, and no one would play them. We played them — before a packed house. We won. We played well. Everyone was excited. The community excitement stemmed from the fact it was a "happening," not because it was basketball.

The Bucknell game tied the record. We played UNLV next, with a chance to set the new record, and we lost — didn't play very well, but again it was a standing-room-only, sellout crowd. A couple of days later, New Year's Day, on national TV with Dick Vitale and the whole grand splash, we played New Mexico — again, sellout crowd, even though there still were no students on campus. We won. The place went wild. My team was happy. I think they enjoyed being a part of all that — they felt, and rightly so, that they were a big part in that record-setting. There was just terrific enthusiasm, a great celebration, as warm and nice a personal tribute as I ever could have received.

But even in the middle of all that, I couldn't help thinking — it wasn't basketball per se, it was a *happening* that brought this about.

What I had sensed before, I knew that day. It was time for me to leave, to find a place that fit me better. Really, it was past time.

Don't get me wrong: I loved people in Lubbock. I loved what it offered me in areas that fit me so well: hunting, fishing, golf — just as I loved people in Bloomington and had fishing, hunting, and golfing pals and places to go.

You can become overwhelmed with sentimental thoughts: *Nice people here, they have been awfully good to me.* But when it comes to life decisions, it's got to be what's best for you and your ability to do your job, not getting swayed by things that have nothing to do with your profession. Comfort enters into decision-making, and that's always dangerous. You have to decide what is the best thing to do, not what is the "right" thing, in a theoretical sense.

KNIGHT'S NUGGETS

I know it's late, but I don't like the looks of that place. We can get a bite to eat in the next town.

If you like gas station vending-machine food.

The road doesn't look icy.

Too late to find out, when the slide starts.

This gun isn't loaded.

How long does it take to make sure?

7

Negative Routes to Big, Big Wins

WHEN I MOVED FROM West Point to Indiana, on the outside it looked like: *Indiana has had outstanding players and teams over a long period of time; basketball is a heavily followed sport all over the state; a lot of great players have come out of the state.* In all those things, it looked like Indiana was going to be a really good coaching situation for me.

But I was married to the idea that defense wins games. Defense was not something that Indiana's basketball teams had ever been widely known for.

I knew I wasn't just asking the players to think in terms of a brand-new priority. To the fans, too, the emphasis I wanted to put on defense and shot selection was totally different from

what they had thought of as Indiana basketball—"Hurryin'
Hoosier" basketball—for not just years but decades.

I had moments of thinking:

What am I getting into?

Can I win in this situation?

I think you play basketball one way. They're used to seeing it
played another way, and they love it.

I was really unsure about the likely acceptance about
the way we were going to play—whether, as I heard later, a
Bloomington guy who became a great friend of mine was
right when he said at the time, "I'm not sure how those 51–50
games are going to go over here." Games in the 50s were not
uncommon when our Army teams were leading the nation in
defense. Halftime scores like that were more the norm at Indiana where, eight times in the decade just before I came, those
"Hurryin' Hoosiers" had won or lost games in which *both*
teams scored 100 points.

But I knew I had to do what I think is best for the kind
of basketball I wanted to play. The coach I succeeded, Lou
Watson, had played in as well as coached that fast-break system, but no one could have treated me better or welcomed me
more openly than Lou did. At several luncheons or dinners,

he introduced me as "the guy who took the hurryin' out of the Hurryin' Hoosiers," and I *liked* that.

I didn't know if it was going to be accepted well by the general public, but I thought then and I always thought at times like that: *What the hell do they really know about it? I think I know more about what it takes to win than anybody in that arena. I have to stick to what it takes.*

My first real test came in my fourth game as Indiana's coach — at Louisville, against Kentucky and Adolph Rupp, my first Indiana-Kentucky game. As an Ohio native who came straight in from coaching at West Point, I'm not sure I had any real idea of how much Indiana and Kentucky people hated each other over the whole issue of basketball supremacy.

I don't know of any two other neighboring states' universities whose keen sports rivalry starts so early — before their players even get to college. The midsummer Indiana-Kentucky All-Star high school basketball series is unmatched in America. Long before there was a Dapper Dan Classic in Pittsburgh or a McDonald's anywhere, this All-Star series started — in 1940 — and more than seventy years later, it's still going. Before they ever played a college game, Ralph Beard, Wah Wah Jones, Clyde Lovellette, Frank Ramsey, Cliff Hagan, Oscar Robertson, Cotton Nash, Terry Dischinger, Dick and Tom Van Arsdale, Louie Dampier, Wes Unseld, George McGinnis,

Jim McDaniel, Bobby Wilkerson, Darrell Griffith, Kent Benson, Jack Givens, Steve Alford, Allen Houston, Glenn Robinson, Damon Bailey—all of them and a whole lot of other future college stars played in that series.

When I arrived in Bloomington, the Universities of Indiana and Kentucky didn't have a long-standing head-to-head basketball rivalry. From 1944–45 through 1964–65, they never played. They had reopened the series and begun an annual matchup by the time I got there, but Indiana hadn't won the game since 1943 and the Hoosier fans were *really* hungry. The 1971–72 game was in Louisville, not Lexington, because Kentucky played its home games in the Indiana series at the biggest arena available to it, Freedom Hall—right across the Ohio River from the part of red-loving, blue-hating Indiana that was most intense about the rivalry.

We had opened my first year with three good victories—over Ball State, Kansas, and Miami of Ohio, all in six days. Those were the first three games played at brand-new Assembly Hall. I felt it was a great beginning for our program, but to those Indiana fans—especially those southern Indiana fans—those schools weren't Kentucky, and those other coaches weren't Adolph Rupp. And here we were going to Louisville to face not just a state-hated rival but the team that probably was the most noted representative in the country of the firebrand basketball Hoosiers loved.

I rode with my team down Interstate 65 across the Ohio River bridge, not knowing if our best player, Steve Downing, was going to be able to play at all. Steve had injured a knee in the Miami game a week before and hadn't had an all-out practice since then.

All Steve did in that game was play as good a game as I've ever had a player play. He played all fifty minutes in a double-overtime game, scored 47 points, and had 25 rebounds. We won, 90–89.

Sometimes positive results come out of negative situations just by sheer willpower. That's what Steve had that night. He was mentally tough enough to overcome a serious condition involving his knee.

After that game, I really never heard a whole lot about 51–50 games again — maybe an occasional "Shoot!" from an impatient old-school Hoosier fan when our kids were living up to my orders and making four passes every possession, but not even many of those. And it *really* tickled me when success started to make converts, and every once in a while I'd hear coming out of our stands: "Come *on,* you guys, play *defense*" ... or "*Dammit,* get a *good* shot."

I'll always be indebted to Steve and that first Indiana team, of course, but even more than that to athletic director Bill Orwig and president John Ryan, the guys who hired me. They took a very questionable step, bringing me in — just thirty years old, a head coach for six years, a good record but without taking any of my teams to the only tournament that mattered in Indiana and the Midwest, the NCAA. I didn't even want to try to explain to them why at Army we actually once turned down an invitation to the NCAA tournament to go to the less prestigious NIT.

Indiana University and its fans hadn't had anybody but a guy from Indiana coach basketball there for almost fifty years, and here I was from Ohio State, a program Indiana people had really hated since my playing years. Bill Orwig and Dr. Ryan simply thought I was the best guy for the job, and so many times that wasn't the priority factor in a decision like that. I remember telling Mr. Orwig, walking up to Dr. Ryan's door, "This is kind of interesting: a Michigan guy [Bill was a great athlete there] hiring an Ohio State guy to coach at Indiana." And they *did* get a lot of static — not only for that, but because I was pretty much an unknown and a lot of bigger names were thrown around as possibilities before I was selected.

Negative Thinking, for a Championship

In looking back to how often I genuinely applied the Power of Negative Thinking to a game plan, the best example I can offer might be the night in Philadelphia in 1976 when — in my fifth year at Indiana — we beat Michigan to win the national championship.

We went into that championship game unlike any other team in NCAA tournament history: having beaten our finals opponent twice during the season. It hadn't happened before, because it was the first time two teams from the same conference ever played in the championship game.

One of our wins over Michigan, the one in Bloomington, was very lucky for us. Quinn Buckner, who had not shot well, made his first bucket of the day in the last minute to get us within two points. Then they missed a free throw, and at our end Jimmy Crews grabbed a missed shot that was going out of bounds and flipped it toward the basket. Kent Benson scored at the buzzer to tie. We played better in overtime and won (72–67), but there's no other word for it: We were really lucky.

Now we were playing that same team for the national championship, and I went about preparation for the game in a very negative way. The first thing I did was go over that Bloomington game film with our players—I went over and over it, talking about how poorly I thought we had played defensively. That was always the key judging issue for me, but we hadn't played at all well offensively, either, and our shooting was terrible. Scott May missed nineteen shots, his career high. Tom Abernethy, Buckner, and Bobby Wilkerson combined were 2-for-22, and we had twenty-one turnovers. We shot .370 that day, compared to .517 for the season—.523 if we take that one game out. Give Michigan's defense credit, but we knew we had to be a much better team in this game than we had been that day.

A coach can go crazy trying to figure out why that "off" game happened. We had beaten Michigan in Ann Arbor earlier, 80–74, but that time we were playing from on top all day — got off to a 16–2 lead and were never caught. Now, the second game comes about a month later in Bloomington, and we hadn't lost to anybody. We're at home, our crowd's going to be great, maybe — coaches always worry about things like this — and our players felt that all we had to do was show up and we'd beat Michigan again. That's never the case. And it wasn't. That was a long, hard day.

Now it was the third game, for the national championship. I've got to develop a positive outcome out of that situation. To do it, I used a negative approach: about how — if *we* were Michigan — we'd have to be thinking we had a good chance to beat Indiana, based on the last game.

My whole approach was: "We can't *play* like we did in that game. Each one of you guys has to play at his *best,* if we're going to win. They are *not* an inferior team." And we were catching them hot. They had reached the finals by burying Rutgers — which was unbeaten and ranked No. 4 — and they had beaten two really good teams in the tournament before that, Notre Dame (23–5, with All-American Adrian Dantley, ranked 7th) and Missouri (26–4, the Big Eight champion ranked as high as

10th). I made sure they were aware of all that — "Here's a team that's playing well. They *have* to think they can beat us."

Then two minutes into the game we lost guard Bobby Wilkerson, the key man in the defense that made that team so great. Bobby hit his head hard on the court, was knocked out, and had to be taken straight to a hospital with a severe concussion.

We didn't play well without him and were behind, 35–29, at the half. At halftime, I didn't bring up Bobby at all — he's gone, we don't need to think about Bobby not being there, although that was a tremendously negative thing. He wasn't just a great player, he was also a close friend to all of them, especially May and Buckner.

But it wasn't a time to be feeling sorry for Bobby or ourselves. That was the time to say, "Hey, the guys in this room have got to do it. And unless we play the way we're capable of playing, we're going to get beat." To turn that into a positive, we had to have great work from not only Jimmy Crews and Jimmy Wisman replacing Bobby Wilkerson, but everybody had to step it up. And we hadn't done that in the first half, so we were behind. It didn't have to be a national championship game for me to approach a situation like that questioning whether "We'll be okay." First: "How the hell can we play so poorly?" And second: "How can we correct this?"

As soon as I walked in, I asked them a question: "Are we

playing as well as we can play? Each of you — ask yourself that question. And then, are you as an individual playing as well as you can play? Okay, what are we doing wrong? We aren't being very sharp in what we're doing. Our cuts and screens lack sharpness. It's execution, boys. If we can't improve our execution on offense . . . and we *can't* let Michigan jump out on us at the start of the second half — they'll be too hard to catch."

Looking back, everything I talked about at the half was all *if*s and *can't*s and *don't*s. I didn't go in there saying, "Hey, boys, we're doing all right," because we *weren't* doing all right. "We're going to be okay" — no, we're *not* going to be okay unless we change some things, and unless we change them drastically and quickly, we're going to find ourselves in a position where we can't catch up to these guys.

I didn't rant and rave. I stuck right to *if . . . unless . . . can't . . . don't.*

We hadn't given up a lot of points: 35 — not so great, but it was within the realm of possibility to win with that defense. But our offense: 29 points . . . "We can't win this game with our offense operating like it did in the first half." There's that word *can't.*

We held our own through 51–51 with ten minutes left, and then everything we said we had to do, we did. We played so well from there on that in the last five minutes, the game was virtually over. An example of our concentration in that last ten minutes was that Buckner, who was not a great free-throw shooter, hit six straight down the stretch. We were doing everything else awfully well, too.

We scored 57 points in the second half. Nobody said anything about it at the time, and I really haven't seen any mention of it since, but that—57 points—set a record that still stands: the most points any team *ever* has scored in either half in an NCAA championship game.

That's amazing to me, because that was not primarily an offensive team. But what a tribute that is to that team and those players: With the utmost pressure on, they played better for a critical stretch and scored more points than any team ever.

Think of that: 35 points in just ten minutes, the ten minutes that determined the championship—35–17 against a very good team that was playing at its absolute best in the tournament.

I had told them just before they went back on the floor at halftime, "We've got twenty minutes to play basketball as well as we can play. If we don't, we'll just be another team that got beat in the NCAA tournament. But if you play the twenty minutes that you're capable of playing—*if*—you'll be a team for the ages. You'll be a team that people will always remember, not just as a national champion but as a team that didn't lose a game."

It's getting close to forty years later now, and nobody since has matched them.

And people — especially Indiana people — do remember. Of course, I recognize this was a game where offense rather than defense carried the day.

An Introduction to Michael Jordan

Negative thinking, even going against some of my own most basic precepts, was a key to winning another NCAA tournament game when all the talent edge appeared to be with our opponent — an exceptionally well-coached opponent, too.

My familiarity with Michael Jordan started when our 1984 Indiana team played against Michael and North Carolina in the first night of the NCAA regional in Atlanta.

We hadn't had a big year, and they had. They were ranked No. 1 in the country at the end of the season, and Jordan was college basketball's Player of the Year. As good as he was, he wasn't all that Carolina team had. This game also was my introduction to another great player, Sam Perkins, who was to be a starter on our Olympic team and then an outstanding NBA player. James Dougherty was young on this team but became a first-round NBA draft pick. Terry Holland, the Virginia coach, had called this North Carolina team maybe the best ever in college basketball.

Negatives came into play prominently in my planning for that game, though not in the way one might have thought — and not at all in the way I talked to my team that week. I don't especially remember, but I've been told I started our first team meeting that game week by going to the blackboard and saying, "We're going to beat North Carolina and this is how." If so, it was unusual, but we had an unusual assignment.

Negative thinking was behind whatever optimism I was portraying. First of all, in that game I was sure we were not going to be able to stop Jordan. And we definitely weren't going to be able to play North Carolina at *its* game — fast. Dean Smith was one of the great coaches in the history of the game. His teams were always well prepared, they always executed well. It was obvious they enjoyed — and were very good at — playing at a fast tempo, and they played that way on both offense and defense.

That first day talking to our team I started with Jordan: "There are two things we *cannot* let him do. We *can't* let him rebound offensively and we *can't* let him go backdoor."

In the game, Dan Dakich, a six-foot-five junior, did a very good job of carrying that mission out.

And of course he had help. That first day I had said, "Now, we are *not* going to stop Jordan at everything, but when he puts the ball on the floor and he looks to make a drive, we've *got* to come in and help with a second defender — as soon as that ball *goes on the floor,* that second defender has *got* to leave his man and move in there." For me, this was really negative stuff: committing two players to stop one from driving.

"We're going to give him the outside shot, because if we try to take that away he's going to have a better opportunity to drive and to rebound — he's going to be able to back-cut and come up with baskets."

Simply, we had to prevent Jordan from doing what he could do best. We had those two priorities: We can't let him back-cut, and he can't get to the board.

Nor could we play our usual *offensive* game.

We were not a team that played at a fast pace, and I didn't think in this game we'd be able to greatly slow this North Carolina team down. We did stress for this game something we were always conscious of: handling the basketball well. We were a very good ball-handling team, but North Carolina under Dean Smith always liked to trap and double-team on defense: A pass is made, guys leave their man to chase the pass and try to trap the man with the ball into making a bad pass. With excellent athletes all over the court, that defensive tactic and the turnovers it produced greatly enhanced what they did offensively.

We changed tactics to combat their strategy. Instead of using our usual cutting and screening offense, we expected each man receiving a pass to know where our other players were situated and to be ready for a quick pass to one of the teammates. Our primary focus on offense that night was to look for the inevitably open man against North Carolina's double-teaming defense. I think that one thing, our ability to handle the ball well, was the biggest reason we were able to pull off a 72–68 upset in that game.

We didn't make very many errors, and we got good shots. Steve Alford was just a freshman in that game, and he scored 27 points—many of them because of their doubling up on the man with the ball, which at times left even him, our best shooter, open.

For me, scaling back my normal emphasis on cuts and screens was the ultimate in negative thinking. I just didn't think that we were going to be able to play our game with great effectiveness against that defense. The result of going away from our strength was so positive on that one night—the beauty of the NCAA tournament is that you don't have to beat a team four out of seven, just once is enough—that we actually were able to score consistently throughout the game and take a fairly commanding lead into the final minutes. Those minutes were long. We missed an exasperating number of free throws in the final minutes but hit enough at the end to withstand a game-closing onslaught by North Carolina.

A Guard in Among the Giants

We had played another outstanding North Carolina team three years earlier in the 1981 NCAA championship game at Philadelphia—back at the Spectrum, the same place where our '76 team had won its championship. There was both a negative situation and some negative thinking involved in that '81 game, which we won, 63–50.

The negative *situation* was much bigger than the ball game. About six hours before the tip-off, outside a hotel in Washington, President Ronald Reagan had been shot.

By the time word of that got out, we were fully locked in to game preparations. I don't think I was even aware it had happened until about three o'clock that afternoon, and by then the White House was sending out every calming message it could—*the President is in no danger, the bullet did no life-threatening damage, he and the nation were very, very lucky* . . .

It turned out that was false. He actually was in close to grave danger from internal bleeding, but—for international security reasons—that wasn't really known until years later. Meanwhile, the Presidents of North Carolina and Indiana had met and decided—based on the positive assurances about Reagan's condition from Washington—that the NCAA championship game should go forward as planned.

What Dean Smith and I couldn't possibly know was how much of a mental distraction all of this was for our players. If the subject of the attempted assassination came up at all in my pregame talking to the team, I'm sure it was just *Hey, we've got a basketball game to play.* I concentrated on the basketball, and I'm sure the players — ours and North Carolina's — did, too. Their youth was important. Despite all the assurances, I don't think they were as affected as a lot of adults were.

The game itself took on an unconventional element. For the only sustained time in his two seasons with us, we played the best guard in the country, Isiah Thomas, in the low post, back-to-the-basket around the foul line, where centers normally play.

It wasn't something we had particularly planned, but we had done it a few times in regular-season games and many times in practice. That was important. Surprise is always a great weapon, if it has been thoroughly practiced. Unpracticed surprises tend to boomerang into disaster.

Isiah was very hard to guard in there — not really used to playing with his back to the basket but fully capable, obviously an outstanding ball-handler, quick in going either way to take the ball to the basket, excellent at passing out of there if a shooter was open on the perimeter.

He had 4 points in the first half, playing in his normal area. The second half he scored 19 points, and we went from a 27–26 halftime lead to win 63–50. Basically, I just didn't think they would be able to handle him inside, and they weren't.

He was named the game's Outstanding Player, and the most commonly cited reasons for that were two steals that he converted into layups opening the second half to establish a better lead for us. But it was his post play as a six-foot-one guard among giants like James Worthy and Sam Perkins (who were future NBA all-stars) that allowed us to use a third guard in the game named Jimmy Thomas. Jimmy did a great defensive job on their other front-court player, Al Wood, who had scored 39 points in the Tar Heels' semifinal win over Virginia. Jimmy did such a good job off the bench in our final two games that he was named to the All-Final-Four team, one of the rare non-starters to get that honor.

With our smaller and faster lineup, we cut down North Carolina's fast break and won the game on defense. For all we got out of Isiah in the post, the players afterward stressed that the defensive matchups had been the difference.

A Weekend of Negative-Thinking Positives

Our third national championship at Indiana represented a whole string of positive results from consciously going against some of my most basic principles of how to play, one of the most difficult decisions any leader can reach — especially one as firm in how-to-play convictions as I am.

This was in 1987 and it involved not one game but two — the semifinal and final games on a Saturday–Monday weekend at the Final Four in the New Orleans Superdome. Each game presented its own dilemma.

In the Saturday semifinals, Syracuse played first on Saturday and had very little trouble beating — for the third time that year — a Big East opponent, Providence. We came on the court next to take on the No. 1-ranked team in the country, UNLV — Nevada–Las Vegas.

Jerry Tarkanian was a tremendous defensive coach, and his '87 UNLV team was very hard to play against on both ends of the court, the "Running Rebels" nation-leading 92.6 scoring average getting the most attention. Over the years, we were a team that normally liked to take its time, to use a cutting and screening offense, to get our best shooters open for shots they would make at least half the time. That was our plan almost every game.

Going against UNLV, we were a good team, a well-respected team — 29–4 going in, and Big Ten co-champions. But we were known that year more for our shooting and our disciplined offense than for our team's usual trademark, defense — not that I had changed preferences, but that's what our strength was that year, shooting.

So the guys in my present role—the "analysts," in newspapers and on TV—had it all reasoned out that our only chance in this game was to play something of a cat-and-mouse game, slow UNLV down to a pace unnerving for them, play with extreme caution, take advantage of this new thing in college basketball that year, the 3-point shot, and the great 3-point shooter we had, Steve Alford. Do that and, oh yes, one other thing: Villanova-style, as in its 1985 championship-game upset of Georgetown, hit just about every shot.

Many a game I've felt exactly that way, that keeping the ball in our hands most of the game was the best way to counter a talented, fast team. But I wasn't thinking that way this time. The more I saw of Vegas on tape, the more I knew that was how we *didn't* want to play them. My thought going into that game was that we couldn't win that way—because of their *defense.*

I felt our best chance was to play their game against their own defense—if we played at a slow tempo, the big athletes playing their very good defense would just engulf us and we'd have a difficult time scoring at all. The more we passed, the more risk we took of getting one picked off. It was negative thinking by me, totally opposite from how I usually based a game plan: I felt we had to play at the pace they liked—very fast—and score a lot of points, while probably giving up a lot.

Now, game plans are fine, but the best game plan is no good

without execution by the players. With any thought of our "four passes" rule temporarily suspended, our kids still disciplined their shot selection well enough to shoot .617 (still a Final Four semifinal record). UNLV was the team that shot threes (a Final Four–record 35, and hit 13 — one of their guards, Freddie Banks, hit a Final Four–record 10 himself).

And our team? We shot four threes all day, all of them by Alford, who hit two and scored 33 points. We gave up 93 points — almost any other game, that would have made me sick — but scored 97 and that totally uncharacteristic score got us on to the championship game.

Great! What a high that was for our kids that night. In college basketball's brightest spotlight, we had beaten the No. 1 team in the country.

But . . .

Our players were tired. Exhilarated. Emotionally wiped out. And we had another game to play. Right away.

For the national championship.

Never was my last game–next game theory — the challenge of putting a big, big win behind immediately and focusing on the next challenge — more severely tested.

It wasn't a problem for *me*. As soon as that UNLV game was over, my only thought was that we still had a game left, and Syracuse was very well coached by Jim Boeheim, who had terrific athletes, too. The Syracuse talent was not as publicized as

UNLV's because of that No. 1 ranking, but three of their start-ers (six-foot-ten forward Derrick Coleman, seven-foot cen-ter Rony Seikaly, and guard Sherman Douglas) all went on to have NBA careers of more than ten years.

I'm a coach. I wanted to go to work on-court right away on preparing for Syracuse and the zone defense that Boeheim teaches better than anyone in America. He always has that zone so well ingrained in his teams that Syracuse for years be-fore that and to this day has always been one of the hardest teams to prepare for.

But I also knew that hard work on the practice floor was the one thing my players, coming off that UNLV game, just could not do. I looked at them in the locker room after that Saturday night game and saw pure exhaustion — elation, but exhaustion. We did not work one physical minute in the forty-eight hours before the national championship game. We met. We went over things we wanted to do. But we didn't work on the court at all. For me, that was the height of negative think-ing: Yes, we need to work on what Syracuse does, but we *can't.*

They played us well. They led most of the last half. Keith Smart made a lot of very good plays that kept us alive down the stretch, one of them fouling the poorest free-throw shooter on court when they led by a point with less than thirty seconds left. It was Coleman, just a freshman at the time but already an outstanding player. He missed, we got the rebound, and . . .

Another negative approach.

Everyone takes a time out at that point — down one point with the clock under thirty seconds and a national championship on the line — to design exactly what the coach wants to do to set up a crucial shot.

We *had* the ball in play, and we had worked all year to be in a position where our players knew what *we* wanted to do, we knew what defense they would be in — *we* were in the best position we could have to decide our fate. And going with what was normal for us, though it was a national championship game, was just fine with me. I've always felt the best way to counter game pressure is normalcy.

A coach can only dream of getting that from all five players on the court under conditions like that. I can offer no better example from the more than 1,300 games I coached than those final seconds of that 1987 NCAA championship game with Syracuse, the one we won 74–73 when Keith Smart won college basketball immortality by hitting a shot with five seconds left.

"The Shot," people call it. I love Keith. He was a great young man to work with, and he has become a great person, an NBA head coach. But that one play was so much more than "The

Shot" that Keith isn't even my own personal hero of the play. Daryl Thomas is. "Who?" you lovers of college basketball lore are saying. And a whole lot of negative-based decisions preceded even Daryl's role.

One basic move against standard thinking: *With the game on the line, get the ball in the hands of your best player.* We had Steve Alford on the floor, the best shooter in the country. We had Keith Smart on the floor, sensational with the basketball those last eleven minutes — he scored 15 points and had two great assists. *With the game on the line* . . . we didn't put the ball in the hands of either of those guys.

A third guard, Joe Hillman, a nonstarter, a mentally tough sophomore who had come to us from California, was the man who brought the ball up the left side, unhurried — clock down to twenty seconds . . .

Fifteen . . .

Everyone knew we wanted to get Alford open, and he ran his cuts into the Syracuse zone, using screens to move to the right side and taking the primary Syracuse attention with him. Don't be fooled; *we* wanted him taking the big shot, too — if he was open. Syracuse made sure he wasn't with great defense.

So Hillman and Smart, handling the ball on top, thought negatively, went away from Alford, and passed the ball inside to Daryl Thomas — the clock under ten seconds now.

Consider Thomas's situation. What kid in America hasn't

dreamed of a chance like that? National championship on the line, one point down, ball in your hands, chance to take the winning shot . . .

Daryl, back to the basket, sized up the situation and didn't like his chances for getting a good shot away against double coverage from Coleman and Seikaly. So he faked a shot and dropped a pass off to Smart, who made a good fake to the middle, then a quick reverse to the baseline to get open for a fifteen-foot shot . . . just normal offense, what we always tried to do.

My whole idea of shot selection was limiting the shots we take to shots that player would normally hit at least 50 percent of the time. That's what made Keith Smart's shot special to me — at the most crucial point of our entire season, he took, and our team got for him, a good shot, a shot he was likely to make. No miracle, no wonder shot, just exactly what we were trying to get. That and all that went into it, certainly including the high-pressure circumstances, made it as good a demonstration as I can offer of my definition of discipline. In this particular sequence, Daryl's pass was the key; Keith's fouling Coleman was second.

And Keith's shot?

"The Shot" — though not a hard shot — was a great one. It went through with a swish and won the national championship, and Keith Smart's launch will always be one of the iconic pictures in NCAA tournament legendry. But there was nothing more important than Daryl recognizing that he could not get a good shot off.

That was the last of so many negative-based decisions by us that weekend that led up to the whole final sequence:

> Running against UNLV to avoid playing our regular offense against their great defense;
> Shunning practice before the championship game to emphasize rest;
> Not taking a time out at the end;
> The ultimate play: unsung Hillman the man who ran the offense, star Alford the one who took defensive concentration with him in cutting through a zone, Thomas passing up an inside shot to get the ball to Smart and set up . . . "The Shot."

That wasn't our best team. That wasn't our most impressive championship run. But it ranks way up there on my favorite executions of the way we wanted to play basketball, under maximum pressure. At its very base: eliminating mistakes.

Speaking of Officials . . .

I'm supposed to be one of the kings of referee-baiting, but it has never been true. Every year, I think our team led the Big Ten in fewest technical fouls. I've heard coaches — and a *lot* of TV experts, some of them ex-coaches — talk of coaches intentionally getting technical fouls to fire up their teams, or to influence future calls, or something else out there in the psycho-logical realm. All I know is one, I didn't get nearly as many technical fouls in my career as most people thought; and two, I *never* intentionally got one, for any reason.

And referee-baiting?

I have a lot of respect for good officials, and they know I think really good officials are priceless. As all rare things are.

Situational Thinking

Now, the 1976 Wilkerson injury, the 1981 Reagan shooting, the 1987 challenge of playing for the national championship with a tired team — those were negative situations, not exercises in negative thinking, and there's a big difference. Handling negative situations in a way that brings positive outcomes is itself an admirable art.

We've all seen examples of the way some people who have been dealt severe physical disabilities somehow overcome them and move right on with their life. People who have lost one sense early in life — usually blindness, but sometimes hearing, or both sight and hearing — often make up for that by tuning up their other senses to remarkable perception. A friend of mine who owned my favorite hunting and fishing equipment store told me about a man he hired once — he was blind, but he ran the store's checkout desk flawlessly.

Once, my friend watched from his office as a woman approached the blind man carrying a rod and reel she was buying for her husband's birthday. When she noticed his blindness, she drew back, not sure what to do, but he realized that and handled it as he always did: "I'll be fine. Just hand me the merchandise you want and I'll take care of you." She did; he took the rod and reel in his hands, and said, "That's a Shakespeare six-foot spinning rod, that'll be twenty-five dollars. And that's a Garcia Mitchell 308 reel, that's another fifteen."

She was amazed. She leaned over to pick up her purse from the floor to pay for the items, and mortified herself by accidentally, loudly passing gas. Blushing, she straightened up, looked around and saw nobody else close, so her composure came back. She pulled out her checkbook and said: "Now, what was that total?"

"Forty-five dollars," the clerk said.

"Wait a minute," she said. "I thought you said forty dollars."

"That," he replied, "was before you added the duck call."

The Art of the Call

Which brings me to how time has changed me. I love to fish. That hasn't changed. I love to hunt — birds, never ground animals. As time has gone on, I've developed a fondness for turkey hunting. The art is in the call, simulating a mating call from a female to a male, and I've become pretty good at it — so good that it has changed the whole sport for me. I can't describe what a great feeling it is to go out on a pleasant spring day, find a perfect spot to set up, and begin the calling. Patiently. Artfully. Then a call comes back! A male has heard and answered. He's on his way. The trick is to keep him coming, to lure him closer, then closer . . . then out in the open, passionately excited about what he thinks is ahead . . . and:

In times gone by, it was *Pow!* I'm a good enough shot that, under the right conditions, which included bringing him close enough, there would be one dead turkey.

But now I'm finding just as much fun, just as much reward, in pulling off the trick of the call, bringing the turkey out in the open moving toward me, and letting the "game" end right there — no shot fired, no kill. None needed. I've already won. I've already ruined the poor turkey's day. I don't need to kill him. I don't like to clean a killed turkey. I don't like to cook one. If I want to eat one, I can go to the store.

KNIGHT'S NUGGETS

Forget a coat — it's going to be warm tonight.

> *Okay, s-s-so I'm not a w-w-weatherman.*

Put your money down, this long-shot horse is a sure thing.

> *Oh well, we can get it all back with this next race.*

8

By Your Pupils...

JULIE ANDREWS, AS ANNA, the British schoolteacher who is hired to tutor the children of the king of Siam in the Rodgers and Hammerstein musical *The King and I,* starts singing "Getting to Know You" with a great lyrical observation:

> *It's a very ancient saying*
> *But a true and honest thought*
> *That if you become a teacher*
> *By your pupils you'll be taught*

Like Anna, I had something important taught — or at least demonstrated — to me once by one of my players.

In the mid-1970s, we were getting ready to play a December game against a very good Notre Da

ger Phelps, a longtime friend of mine, h

riety of presses. We had scouted them

the specific, different ways we wanted

presses. In practice the week of the ga

who had done the scouting for that game, Bob Donewald, was

on the floor with our players simulating Notre Dame, show-

ing our starters what they had to look for in order to recognize

which press was being applied against us.

One of the starters, Quinn Buckner, had been rotated out

while we were working on a particular teaching segment, and

I was standing by him. After a few moments of listening and

watching, he said, "Coach, can *you* tell the difference in those

presses?"

It wasn't a wiseass remark at all. I knew immediately what

one of the smartest players I ever coached was saying, more

than asking: It *was* hard to spot the difference, with very lit-

tle time to do it, which could lead to potential confusion and

mistakes. Almost immediately after he asked the question, I

had Donewald stop things and told our players, "Here's what

we're going to do, whatever their press is."

We went to one basic plan, which enabled us to play effec-

tively against those four presses and have just one turnover

against them in winning the game — because Buckner recog-

nized a negative issue: He was having trouble spotting a criti-

...rence quickly enough. And he had the intelligence to ...ne great question.

As the Buckner suggestion showed, one of the greatest feelings you can have as a coach is when one of your players remembers something in your coaching and does something that you haven't asked him to do.

Almost a basketball generation after Buckner, we had our team playing in Albuquerque for a spot in the 1992 Final Four. We were playing UCLA, which three months earlier had beaten us on a neutral court at Springfield, Massachusetts, in our season opener, 87–72. Usually repeat matchups have little bearing to me: This is an all-new game, under totally different circumstances, in this case with considerably higher stakes. But this time there was one carry-over memory.

At a luncheon the day of the earlier game, the speaker was my good friend, the late Celtics coach Red Auerbach, who from the podium told the UCLA team how lucky they were to be playing us then — it would be a lot tougher later after this Indiana team had played a full season, Red said. We *were* much better this time, but UCLA hadn't done badly since that game either, going on to win the Pac-10 championship, have a 28–4 season, and get the No. 1 seed over us in this regional.

I've rarely had a team respond better to a challenge than that Indiana team did that day. It started the day before. We had had a tough physical game against Florida State on Thursday night. On Friday, the day between the games, we had a practice time available to us at the game site, but I asked them as a team, "Do you want to practice, or would you rather rest?" I knew our players wanted to do everything they had to do to win, but I also trusted their honesty. Greg Graham was the upperclassman who spoke right up: "Coach, I think we'd be better off resting."

The next afternoon, we jumped on UCLA at the start and kept rolling through halftime, up 44–29.

The Psychological Game

In the final minutes of that very well-played first half, a thought came to my mind about a little psychological game I wanted to play. At "The Pit" in Albuquerque, to get from the court to the locker rooms, both teams had to go up the same long upstairs ramp. An official's call right at the end of the half occupied my attention enough that I expressed my feelings about it and forgot what I wanted to do with the players.

But I looked up and saw that somehow Calbert Cheaney, the veteran leader on that team, had read my mind. Calbert led our guys on a dead sprint past the UCLA guys all the way up the ramp, looking as fresh as if the game hadn't even begun. Already down 15 points and looking at how fresh our guys obviously were, I know those UCLA players had to be thinking, "You've got to be kidding." Our guys came out for the second half that fresh, too, and ran off to a 106–79 win that probably is as much of a trouncing as a really good UCLA team ever took in the tournament. And Calbert did that halftime sprint entirely on his own.

Calbert Cheaney might be the first example that comes to my mind in refuting another of those questionable axioms that someone said once and we've blithely accepted ever since: *Leaders are born, not made.*

The Calbert Cheaney who came into our program was an excellent basketball player, easily the best in an outstanding group of freshmen, but he was a long way from a leader — a very quiet kid who worked at developing himself as a leader and became one of the best senior captains I ever had. He was also one of the best players — College Player of the Year his senior year, and still the holder of the career scoring record for Big Ten players almost twenty years after he graduated. I remember a lot of his outstanding basketball contributions, but nothing else makes me smile inwardly the way I do when I think of the halftime dash he took our team on to wordlessly give UCLA the old show-business teaser "You ain't seen nothin' yet."

Fallacy of First Impressions

Calbert also disproved another of those axioms we continually hear: *First impressions are lasting.*

I don't reject that one altogether. I think it is important in pursuit of a job or in introduction to someone that you do your absolute best to come across well — not falsely, but at your best. With Calbert and me, it wasn't a matter of grooming in how he looked to me the first time I saw him. I had heard very good reports on this left-handed forward who played way down in the southwestern tip of the state at Evansville Harrison High School, so I flew down to watch his team play at home against Jasper. A great shooter, I had heard. That night, he shot poorly and too often — I always say he was 3-for-20, he says, yeah, it was bad, but more like 7-for-25 — and maybe he was right with his numbers for the game, because I was so unimpressed and so far from home I left after the third quarter. I told my staff and his coach that we wouldn't be recruiting him.

That was in February. That summer, I was talking with my staff, going over guys we wanted to get in what was an unusually good year of prospects in Indiana, when one of them said, "I know you saw him and didn't like him, but the best guy out there right now is Calbert Cheaney." We looked again, felt he was a recruit we really wanted, got back on him, and got him.

That one experience removed forever whatever tendencies I might have had toward that "first impressions are lasting" baloney. One look, one glance can't always tell you everything you need to know in sizing up a basketball recruit or potential employee. When there is any doubt, continue to look—and be willing to change your mind, if there is a reason to.

Calbert Cheaney's further development after he arrived at IU as already a good prospect is not an exception. Maybe as a coach, as a leader, you will come across someone who does everything so well there is nothing really to work on, to get better at. I never found such a person, and I had Michael Jordan on the 1984 Olympic team. Michael was outstanding, the best player I ever coached, but he wasn't a *great* shooter . . . yet. He was a great athlete, exceptional at scoring, rebounding, playing defense, running the floor, doing just about everything that makes a great basketball player. As a pro, he developed his shooting to greatness. Obviously, it wasn't something he *couldn't* do. It took work, and with that he turned a negative into a positive, as did Calbert Cheaney in the area of leadership.

If It Ain't Broke, Fix It

I have always felt that a coach with a negative approach to a game will be more likely to make better midgame or late-game changes—"adjustments," in TV talk—than the positive thinker, who I believe has a tendency to stay too long with the way he thought—he *knew*—would be good enough to win.

The "if it ain't broke, don't fix it" axiom is much too positive for me, because the end of a game is completely different for me in some important tactical ways. Clair Bee, whose .826 career winning percentage is the best in college basketball history, told me he liked to have his team a point or two behind at halftime, because "when they're behind, they listen better." I never went quite that far; I preferred to be ahead whenever I could be.

But I understood his point. One of the toughest situations I ran into as a coach was going to halftime after my team had played so well in the first half it had opened up a big lead — and nothing lasted with me more than the bitter taste I had in the thankfully few games when we did build up a 15- or 20-point lead by halftime and then let it get away with poor second-half play and lost. There aren't many, but games like that stick in my mind.

Experiences like those were why I was *never* a "Way to go, guys!" coach after a well-played first half. Even after the best of first-half performances by my teams, I *always* found something to point out that they could have done better, or they really had to watch out for in the second half. Several years ago I did a TV commercial for Minute Maid where my team came in at halftime after obviously playing well, and I greeted them with a big smile and cookies and nice words. I had to go to Los Angeles two days early just to prepare for that one. I got paid well for it, but that performance should have won me an Oscar.

Whatever the score, I always emphasized that the first five minutes of the second half are the most important of the whole game. Very, very often that *is* the period that sets the tone for the rest of the game, and many times — unless the halftime score is clear out of whack — that is when a game swings.

The moral I got out of those games that got away was: Never accept just playing well. Always strive to play even better.

Winning the Team Fouls Race

Timing is everything. That's an adage I don't quarrel with, because it is true in any kind of leader's operating procedure.

The last five minutes of a basketball game has its own separate importance. Whatever our game plan had been up to then, if we were ahead in the last five minutes of a game, I wanted us to use that lead and make the clock our teammate. I wanted to forget about taking three-point shots . . . to eliminate quick shooting, period . . . to think less about jump shots and try to drive the ball to the basket and get layups or free throws. I consider getting to the free-throw line at the end of close games the most important key to winning those games.

That is, essentially, a negative approach: When we have the ball and a lead late in a game, our biggest objective is *not* scoring. We're not in a hurry, we're going to kill some clock, pull our guys up off the baseline, clear the floor to give our ball-handlers room, and look to drive the ball — to get a chance every time to draw a foul *and* possibly score a basket, or make a drop-pass to an open man. The more time we took, the more anxious losing teams became. Anxious people make a lot of mistakes, and we shot a lot of free throws.

In any game, I always wanted my team to win the team fouls battles, to be the first to shoot one-and-ones (after the sixth foul on a team each half), and the first to shoot an automatic two free throws (after the ninth foul each half). I think that's one of the most overlooked and most important aspects of a college game, because it doesn't just put points on the board but also accumulates fouls on the individual players who wind up on the bench. Time lost on the bench by key opponent players was of incalculable value for us (and vice versa). This was one of the hidden keys to winning that occur in any competitive endeavor.

Always, when the first postgame box score was handed to me, the first thing I always looked at was how many free throws we shot and how many our opponents shot. Our objective, not just every game but every year, was to make more free throws than our opponents shot. To do that covers a multitude of good team achievements. And to facilitate that, one of our most important basic drills was playing defense with the hands inside the belts — out of use. Defense is played with the feet, with positioning.

The Hidden Values of Drawing Fouls

That wasn't something I was conscious of as a player. My junior year at Ohio State, our team played a December game against St. John's in Madison Square Garden—the Holiday Festival in New York—and I was being guarded by their All-American, Tony Jackson. I drove the lane and made a bucket against Jackson, which was a big thrill for me.

The basket was disallowed, because he fouled me on the drive to the basket—and I was *really* disappointed, because I lost that bucket I had scored—against Tony Jackson!

I was given a one-and-one free-throw opportunity, and I hit both free throws. But boy, I hated losing that basket against an All-American.

Years later I thought back on that with a completely different perspective. Our team lost the two points on the disallowed basket, but we got them back on the free throws—and it was a foul on Jackson, which got him one foul closer to foul trouble.

As a player, you don't really understand everything that's important. So when I started coaching, I went over that one situation in my mind—where I was so disappointed about losing the basket and wasn't even thinking about how much better that play was for our team because of the foul. That one personal memory was a big reason for my lifelong theory on free throws: the value of shooting more free throws than the opponents did; getting into a one-and-one situation faster than they did; getting to a two-free-throw situation faster; and accumulating fouls on their key players, which would put them on the bench.

Teaching, Teaching, Teaching

Even the best teams occasionally run into a game when important free throws are missed, sometimes in bunches, and inevitably some of their fans go out into the night grumbling, "They must not even *practice* shooting free throws."

Well, all teams do, but the search forever has been for the most effective way to really simulate game conditions and pressures to make the practice more effective. And the truth with most teams and coaches probably is that not enough practice time *is* spent on free-throw shooting, or emphasizing the value of the free throw, or figuring out the most effective way of really practicing shooting free throws as if it were in a game.

In practice, my teams shot them as almost every other team does: as an end to practice. But I'd also do things like pull one player out in front of all the others and say, "All right, Quinn, you've got a one-and-one — make both of them or everybody

BOB KNIGHT

has to run five sprints." That's not a tremendous penalty, but it puts a little peer pressure on, because his teammates really get on a guy who misses.

Much more commonly, in a hard practice I had my teams shoot free throws as a rest break when I felt one was needed. We'd go at it hard for about twenty minutes, and I'd always try to pick an upbeat time — after a particularly good execution of what we were trying to get across. That's when I'd stop things by yelling, "Free throws!" Because of the timing, this usually communicated to my players that I was happy with what I had just seen.

Our procedure at those breaks was that groups of usually two would go to the various baskets around the practice court, each player would shoot two free throws each, and then that group would rotate after maybe five minutes. I always felt that accomplished several things: a needed break, of course, and a shot of confidence because something had just been done well by our team. Plus they were practicing shooting free throws while they were tired, as happens when they're fouled during a game.

They weren't up there just to shoot; they were expected to simulate game pressure and try to hit each shot. Also, for the ones not shooting, there's a mental break as they line up to rebound — "Free throws!" meant a chance to catch a breath,

which I hoped would have carryover value in the same re-
freshing break at such interruptions during a game. At least,
I *hoped* that was the mental association they got out of a free-
throw break before another twenty minutes of all-out practice.

The absolute best way to get a good team free-throw percentage is to have your best shooters taking the free throws.
That's not really joking. That is the challenge of coaching:
getting shots (the source of most free throws) for your best
shooters, keeping the ball out of the hands of poor passers or
shooters, generally accomplishing the obvious as often as possible.

But my free-throw-practice theories were no different from
my basic intent for every phase of practice. I wanted my teams
and my players to put something into and get something out
of every minute on that practice floor, that classroom. And,
just like a classroom, I wanted them to know that I felt each
player's ability to think — to concentrate on winning — was
very important.

That applied to everybody on the roster, not just the starters or the ones likely to do the most playing in a game. I felt it
was my job as coach to let each player know what he could do
to help the team win, even if it's just as a practice player. And
we won some games, definitely some championships, because

of what players that nobody in the crowd associated with winning games did to extend our starting players into game-type effort on the practice court.

I got a special kick after our 1981 NCAA championship hearing Isiah Thomas single out Chuck Franz, his usual practice court matchup, and others on our backup team for their contribution to that championship. Only the players and coaches, who are lucky — and demanding — enough to get that effort from everybody on a team, know how vital practice-time is. I considered it my most important job as a coach to let every player know when he had made a contribution to winning.

A Matter of Time

Time is a negative factor too often overlooked. The leader must look at any project with full understanding of what will be required — including how much *time* — to get things done right, to be ready for the first real test. A coach, a player, an ambitious salesperson or office employee has to understand he can't do everything to achieve an objective in a few days — maybe even in a year. Experience and understanding come into play there, along with discretion about talking too much and promising too much, which is a problem for a lot of people in sports — many of them coaches.

One time my basketball team was getting ready for a road

game, and while my players were on the court at our shoot-around the morning of a key road game, the football coach at the school — whom I knew through a couple of golf events — came in and sat down beside me. If it had been a practice, I wouldn't have been sitting or talking, but shoot-arounds were a little different, so we talked. He had been at this traditional football power school for a few years, and he was beginning to feel concerned about keeping his job. He asked me, "Bob, what do you think I need to do differently?"

I liked him, so I was straight with him: "First of all, you've got to quit playing up your recruits so much. You keep telling your fans you're getting the greatest quarterback in the country or the greatest something-else, and after a while of course they expect all those great recruits to make a great team. Just keep your mouth shut." He nodded very seriously, and said, "You're absolutely right, Bob. That's really good advice."

It wasn't five minutes later when the recruiting season under way at the time came up in our conversation — my fault this time, because I realized what time of the year it was. With honest curiosity, I asked, "By the way, how did your recruiting go?" And he replied, "Bob, we're getting the number-one player out of California and the number-one player out of Texas and out of New Jersey . . ." I just rolled my eyes.

That was twenty years ago. Just recently, I had a late-summer conversation with a hometown friend of mine who is one of that school's big fans. "How're they going to be this fall?" I asked him. He had been down that path many times. His answer: "Well, if we're half as good as this coach says we're going to be, we'll be all right." And they were upset in their opener. Some people, some professions, never learn.

KNIGHT'S NUGGETS

One more beer can't hurt.

Unless you're driving.

Don't worry, there are never any troopers on this road.

It only takes one. Cut the speed and save —
some money, or your license.

9

A Time to Aim High

I NEVER WANTED THE players I coached—even those with exceptional talent, including Michael Jordan and the other members of the 1984 U.S. Olympic team—to think that their individual abilities were all they needed to win a championship. I wanted them to learn how to best use their great talent. I wanted them to understand what it took to be successful in competition—to win. It takes the mind as much as those great physical skills, maybe even more so.

If—as I did once in my coaching life—you have one of those years when you do see that you have the makings of an outstanding team, don't say, "Our goal is to go unbeaten." Better to say: "The only thing that will satisfy this team to its full extent is to be undefeated. We have to do what we can do within the limitations of our abilities, and we have to play that way for forty minutes."

That's exactly what I told my 1975–76 Indiana team before our first practice of the year, the only time I ever set a goal like that in front of any of my teams, and those kids lived up to it through what is — still, almost forty years later — the last time a team stood as major college basketball's undefeated champion.

I remember one other meeting with those 1975–76 players, one unlike any I ever had, because I was talking to players who had done something no Big Ten basketball team had ever done: completed two straight undefeated regular seasons, including one that was 36–0. When I called them together in the locker room before we went out for our first practice the day after the regular season ended, I'm sure they were expecting a refocus, a reminder that our 31–0 record didn't carry any weight now, that everybody in the tournament was starting out 0–0, that kind of thing.

That wasn't what they got. The best team in America got its ears blistered. I didn't let anyone into the locker room but the players and me — no assistant coaches, no managers, nobody. I really drilled them about things I had observed, about hours they were keeping — I just raked them over the coals. I wanted to put them in a position where for the next few weeks there damned well wasn't going to be *any* interference. They had to go to class and they had to play, and that's all I wanted them to think about it for the next three weeks.

Through it all, I didn't mention any names.

After I was done, I went out onto the court to wait for them to come out for practice. I can remember the whole scene perfectly, all these years later: I'm standing, leaning against the basket support, when I hear one basketball dribbling. The first guy out: Scott May. Two-year All-American. Great player.

He just walks past me, dribbling that basketball. Then he turns around, looks at me, and says: "That was good, Coach. I think they got the message."

That was one of the great things I ever heard a kid say: "I think *they* got the message."

He didn't think one thing I said had pertained to him. And he was right. It didn't.

And that team was pretty good. *Really* good.

My All-Time MVP

Every kid on a basketball team grows up shooting. Not every kid *is* a shooter.

Maybe no player I ever had exemplified that more than one of the least-honored starters on our great 1974–75 and 1975–76 teams at Indiana. Bobby Wilkerson was the lowest-scoring starter for those teams, but he was the most valuable player I ever coached. He played his role better than anyone I ever had.

It was about the most versatile role I ever gave a player, because Bobby's physical abilities were enormous — six-foot-seven, wiry-strong, exceptional jumper. He actually jumped for us at the game-opening tip-off, and we had a six-foot-ten All-American center, Kent Benson. In the 1976 NCAA Final Four semifinals against UCLA, guard Bobby Wilkerson had 19 rebounds — I'm sure that's a Final Four record for guards, although they probably don't keep such a thing. And he did it on a floor with six front-court players — three for them and three for us — who all played in the NBA.

Bobby wasn't a great shooter, but he recognized that and still had some big scoring nights. And he led that team — maybe the best-passing team that ever won a national championship — in assists.

All that doesn't even mention his greatest strength: defense. He could stop anyone — a forward, a center, a guard. Whoever we put him on he went along with it. One of the few coaches who recognized what he gave us was the guy I grew up with in the same Ohio county, Bill Musselman, who started as Minnesota's head coach the same year I went to Indiana.

We were both in our fourth Big Ten seasons when Wilkerson came along and started playing all the roles he did. Musselman pinpointed that tip-off assignment and told me: "I don't even know if he's your best guy to do that, but don't tell me you don't realize what seeing that does to the guard he's going to be covering." I never dealt much in psyching guys out — Bobby jumped center for us because he *was* our best at it. But I think Musselman had a point.

Wilkerson didn't go unrecognized. He never made an All-Big Ten team, but he was the eleventh player taken on the first round of the 1976 NBA draft — probably about as high as any guard ever went who averaged 8 points a game. And he had a good, long NBA career.

The '75 team was strong all around, but its heart was the guard combination of Buckner-Wilkerson. The best player on the team was Scott May, who was the leading scorer and College Basketball Player of the Year. Scott was as good a player as I ever had because he had the fewest negatives of any player I ever coached. By his senior year, he had eliminated them; he rarely made mistakes. In general, the 1974–75 and 1975–76 teams were my best teams because they played the game with the fewest errors. They didn't beat themselves and virtually nobody else did either.

Our '76 team won a national championship, but many of the players and I felt that the '75 team was actually better because we had two strong senior shooters — Steve Green and John Laskowski.

The '76 team is always rated in the top three of all-time best teams, along with UCLA's 1968 and 1972 teams. The consensus is UCLA '68 (with Lew Alcindor/Kareem Abdul Jabbar) was the all-time greatest, our '76 team second and UCLA '72 third. I'm not sure our team could have beaten the Alcindor/Jabbar team. This is a case where they had superior talent so that if they played their normal game and we did the same, we'd probably have lost. Of course, I would have tried to find a way to beat them — that's the fun part of coaching. I always believed it would have been a great coaching opportunity to prepare for a game like that: The tougher the opponent, the harder the challenge.

You can bet we would have tried.

My Clark Gable Approach

I was always seen as a coaching dictator: If there was a decision to be made, *I* made it.

I can't imagine how that got started, because it wasn't true. One of the self-governing aspects of coaching that I always practiced on myself was: Don't get caught up with those things that are just immaterial, that don't make any difference in winning or losing.

I always let my players vote on everything I didn't care about — where we would eat on a road trip, whether we would practice at three or five o'clock — everything that didn't make any difference toward winning, I let them vote on, so they felt they had a voice.

But we never elected a captain. *I* picked the captain. MVP? At the end of the season, I always picked that, too. Those are things that I felt could make a difference in winning games, immediately or in the future.

However, that whole idea of getting caught up in things that are a waste of time . . .

Clark Gable's line in *Gone with the Wind* — "Frankly, my dear, I don't give a damn" — is my idea of about how those things should be handled.

In one of my years at Indiana, we had just beaten Wisconsin in a close game. A lawyer from northern Indiana wrote to me, upset about how we played — we didn't do this and didn't do that. We had beaten Wisconsin thirty-some times in a row, so I wasn't questioning our approach all that much, but mostly for my own amusement I wrote him back and said: "You have to understand one thing: I've always operated under the theory that if Abraham Lincoln couldn't please all the people all the time, I couldn't, either."

Three days later I get a letter back from the guy: "You have to understand: I didn't like Lincoln, either."

All that experience did was give me a pen pal, and I hadn't

made any progress on avoiding time-consuming diversions. So when I was talking once with the great Texas football coach Darrell Royal, he got onto the subject of using time well — how time that is wasted because you're involved in things that aren't important shortchanges things that are. I thought about my exchange with the lawyer and asked Darrell how he handled mail. He said his secretary read every piece of mail he got, and she threw all the garbage away. He answered the ones she forwarded. Sounded good to me, so I went to that system.

After that, people would come up to me and say they had written me a letter, and I would have some fun: "Oh, my secretary reads all my mail, and everything worthwhile she sends on to me and I answer. Did you hear back from me?" And with that setup line, I'd *always* hear, "Oh . . . *I* got an answer from you." Always. I *never* heard anybody say they didn't.

Looking and Seeing — Confessing Is Optional

Sherlock Holmes was fond of saying, "Many people look but few see." A great word is *observation*. See what's there. Be observant.

You never know the rewards you can get for nothing more complex than that.

Karen and I were driving in the hills of Alabama, enjoying the gorgeous scenery, and I said, "Turn on the radio to

FM 93.5. It's a great country-western station." She turned it on just in time to hear what she knew was one of my favorites, Johnny Horton singing "The Battle of New Orleans," and she said, "How did you *know* that?" I said, "I've been here before — about ten years ago. I just remembered how good that station was." She couldn't believe what an amazing memory I had.

Eventually, I confessed. About a half-mile before I asked her to turn the radio on, while she was reading a book or magazine and I was looking around driving, we passed a sign that Said GREAT COUNTRY AND WESTERN MUSIC, 93.5.

She's too smart to ever fall for that one again, but by just being observant I had at least a few moments of reward.

The Patton Approach

As a basketball teacher, I became used to giving my "students" tests before 16,000 people, many of whom each time really saw it as a test of me. So speaking before good-sized crowds has never carried any particular fear for me. Never at any of my "tests" did I really feel I was trying to sell anything — just to win basketball games. I felt a little different when I was part of a speakers' group at a motivational leadership conference, and the big name of the group spoke before me. In eleven minutes he mentioned fifteen times the tapes and books he had for sale in the lobby.

I couldn't resist. When my turn came, I said, "I don't have any tapes or books or anything else to sell to you, but I have spent a long time working in front of 16,000 people, and I can tell you the difference between winning and losing." I didn't make any money with that line, but I did smile inside about the dig I got in to the previous speaker whose idea of motivation was motivating people to give him cash.

Stories are one of the best ways to communicate and sometimes even motivate, because they paint a picture that sticks in a listener's mind. I heard one about leadership involving the World War II general I admire so much, George C. Patton — who knows if it's true? I like to think it was.

Patton and his driver were on a desert road in Africa when a German plane came on them suddenly and strafed them. Patton and the driver scrambled out of their jeep and dove in a ditch. From there Patton looked up and saw a soldier on a telephone pole, oblivious to the flying bullets, eyes fixed on the wires he was working with, locked in on his job.

Patton, concerned for the soldier's safety, yelled out, "What the hell are you doing up there, soldier?" The Pfc. didn't look down, and with no thought of rank or insolence or anything military yelled back, "I'm trying to fix this goddamn wire if you'll let me alone."

"Son," Patton said, "you're doing a hell of a job."

That's a leader and a good listener to his troops.

Driving Home a Point

A teenage boy felt the time had finally come when he should be getting the family car. He saw his dad sitting in his favorite chair and went up to him.

"Dad, did Mom tell you that I passed the driver's license test today?"

"Johnny, she *did* tell me. And not only that, she said the state trooper who gave you the examination said you had the highest score of anybody he had ever tested. I think that's great! That's a real accomplishment. I'm proud of you."

"Well, Dad . . . now can I use the car once in a while?"

The father thought a minute and said, "Now, John, I knew this day would come, and I've thought about it a lot. I've been watching you, and here's what I've decided. First, there are some things you have to change.

"Number one, your grades have to improve. That last grading period was just unacceptable for a kid with your intelligence. That's your first objective.

"Second, your mom has been complaining a lot the last few weeks about how you're treating your younger brother and sister and how uncooperative you have been with her — you've just been kind of a pain in the ass, and that has to stop.

"Number three, John, you know I've told you ever since you've been in school that you don't read nearly enough —

that reading is the key to all education, and education is vital to success, and here you are a junior in high school and you aren't a bit better about that. That's going to change. I want you to start reading, and not just popular stuff, I want you reading the Bible — not only for its religious significance but also because there's a lot of really good guidance in the Bible.

"And, John, there's a fourth thing: You've *got* to get a haircut. I'm tired of that damn long hair — I've told you about it before, and I'm through asking. That's an ultimatum now: Do it or you don't drive the car.

"You do those four things and *then* we'll sit down and work out a way for you to use the car."

About three weeks later, Johnny saw his dad sitting in his chair watching a ballgame, and he went up to him and said, "Well, Dad, I'm ready to talk to you again about using the car. I think I've done those things you said I had to do."

His dad turned away from the game, looked at him, and said: "John, let me tell you, your grades *have* improved drastically, which means you were being lazy before, but this is good. I'm telling you, though, those grades had better not slip.

"Secondly, and even more important, your mom tells me you have been very helpful to her around the house, and you've even been good to your brother and sister — she's really pleased with you. I like that.

"Also, I've noticed myself that every night you've got a book or a magazine in your hands, and you're *reading* them. That's great, John. I'm sure you have learned a *lot.* And every once in a while I've seen you leafing through the Bible and actually reading sections of it.

"So, John, those three things you've done extremely well.

"But you still haven't cut that long damn hair."

Johnny was ready. "Dad, I wanted to talk to you about that. In reading the Bible, as you told me to do, I noticed that Peter, Matthew, Mark, Luke, John — even Jesus himself — they *all* had long hair."

"Yes they did, Johnny," he said, "that's exactly right. And did you notice, too, that everywhere they went, they walked their asses off?"

KNIGHT'S NUGGETS

Oh, I can shovel all this snow alone.

> *Maybe you'd better (gasp!) call an ambulance.*

I don't need anyone holding the ladder for me.

> *Anyone know the closest hospital?*

10

"You're Representing Your Country"

T HE MOST SATISFYING THING I did in my forty-some years in coaching was coaching the United States team in international basketball competition, and I was lucky enough to get to do it twice — with the team that won the 1979 Pan American Games gold medal at San Juan and an altogether different group that was the last American amateur team to win the Olympic gold medal at Los Angeles in 1984.

Henry Iba, the great former Oklahoma State coach who was the U.S. coach at three Olympics, prepared me well with one sobering advisory: *This time you won't be coaching a team for your school or your state. You're representing your country.*

I knew that meant a lot to him, and it certainly did to me.

I've worked into speeches at hundreds of appearances since the Olympics what I told that team more than once: The eight greatest words ever written are "America, America, God shed His grace on thee."

Within that was another experience of equal interest and equally as fond a memory: the opportunity to coach Michael Jordan, who I think without any reservation went on to be not only the greatest player in the history of the game of basketball but also the best player ever to play in any team sport. His competitiveness, his abilities, his desire made him such.

It Started with 74

My procedure each time was the same, though of course the Olympics bring a much bigger spotlight.

I learned that I was going to be the 1984 Olympic coach in May 1982. I went to work almost immediately, building files on possible players — ours and the ones we would be facing. Keep in mind, in those days, our team was made up of college players.

Once we had a squad and it was time to start practice as a team, we did things the Knight way. We had great players on each team, but we started practice as though they were trying out for their junior high team. The message was clear: Their reputations had nothing to do with how we were going to play.

I wanted them to know we were going to do just what Frank Sinatra sang about: *my way*. And I think the players on those teams worked harder than any teams that have ever represented us in international play.

With Jordan and the Olympic team, days after the 1984 Final Four in Seattle we brought seventy-four kids to Bloomington for the trials. We cut it to thirty-two, to twenty, to sixteen, and finally to the twelve we took to Los Angeles.

At the first meeting with those twelve in the locker room at Assembly Hall, I talked to them about what was going to be important to us as a basketball team.

I said, "You guys have to have a faith in us, that we're going to prepare you. If you don't think you're the best-prepared for a basketball game you've ever been, I want you to tell me about it, because we have to do something to make sure that you are. You have to have a belief that we will have you prepared.

"And we have to have a feeling about you twelve that you're going to do what we want done. There has to be a rapport between coaches and players — a feeling for one another, a combined effort toward an eventual goal, so that on the night of August 10, each one of you twelve will be standing on a platform, with our national anthem being played and a gold medal around your neck.

"That's what this is all about."

I gave every kid a 3 x 5 photograph of an Olympic gold medal. "I want this in your pocket, whatever you have on, wherever you go, until the real thing is yours."

I gave them all an 8 x 10 copy of the same picture. "I want this over your bed wherever you sleep between now and then."

The last week of training, when we were in San Diego getting ready to go to Los Angeles, I had Alex Groza speak to our team. Alex was on the Kentucky teams that won the NCAA championships in 1948 and '49, and as a result of that '48 championship was selected to play on our Olympic team that won the gold medal in London in 1948. Alex was living in San Diego. When we were out there to play our last pre-Olympics game, he came to practice one morning and brought his gold medal along.

He had made it into a necklace for his wife. I remember Alex passing that gold medal around to our players and each kid looking at it, and each kid thinking about what he was going to do with his. I could just see it in their faces: Each kid held it, and each kid was reluctant to pass it on to the next kid, till all twelve of them had held that gold medal.

When they gave it back to Alex, I said, "How many of you gave a thought as to what you want to do with your gold medal and who you want to give it to?"

Everyone grinned.

And every kid raised his hand.

And today, every one of those "kids" has a gold medal.

Summer Basketball Before 67,596

As for playing against someone other than ourselves, everything started for that 1984 Olympic team with a nine-game exhibition series against NBA stars, including a night I'll never forget in an atmosphere I'll never see again.

It was at Indianapolis in the football Hoosier Dome, where the Olympians played against an NBA All-Star team that included home-state favorites Larry Bird and Isiah Thomas. This was part of a 9–0 sweep that prepared our team well for the Olympic competition in Los Angeles.

It wasn't just our team that was on display that night. Coach Pat Summitt's Olympic women's team played in the first game, ahead of us. I thought it was great — really good for Pat's team and our team. Pat and I had been the U.S. basketball coaches in the 1979 Pan American Games, and our teams won gold medals there, too. The summer of '79 leading up to the Pan American Games was my first real association with her, and she really impressed me. Pat is very tough-minded. She has meant a lot to the game of basketball — not just the women's side of the game, *basketball.*

Our objective that first night was to see if—in July, in a new building where they had to figure out a way to put a basketball court in the middle of the vast football field that it was built for—basketball-loving Indiana could turn out what we wanted: the biggest crowd ever to see a basketball game in America.

It happened—67,596 people—and not for more than a dozen years, after several years of playing the NCAA Final Four in domes around the country, was that number topped.

That night had all the feeling of a spectacle, more than a game. It was the first athletic event ever in the brand-new Hoosier Dome in Indianapolis, built for the Indianapolis Colts, not for basketball. But this was a state that loved basketball more than it did the Colts—at least at that time—and this night brought out all the star-spangled feeling American basketball fans have toward the team that represents them in Olympic competition.

And then it was game time. While putting the team together during practice, we moved the lineups around a lot. Everybody played against everybody else. And going into these first exhibition games, I didn't know what to expect.

I wanted us to play against the best players of the world, the NBA players, just to see what that was like. It's different than playing college basketball. What might be a negative for us—

our exposing these kids to the pros — could really be a positive, if we could hold our own. No question: I wanted to win. I
felt beating the pros would be a great confidence builder.

It worked out that we did win. We won that night, as we
had in our first game at Providence, and then won again and
again. The NBA guys were great. We drew great crowds all
across the country, and as we won, those NBA guys came after
us harder and harder, and I felt that it did an awful lot for our
team.

I worked my ass off from selection to the medal. I always
worked the players hard the next day after every game. I
looked upon them as going through basic training, to blend
their skills into a team. I wanted them to never be satisfied until they got the medal.

A Golden Night in Los Angeles

Whenever I had a team that I felt had a chance to accomplish
something far superior to what others could, I laid that out for
them — and I had done that right from the start with our 1984
Olympic team. I wanted them to know what was at stake.

They responded as well as I could have hoped. But still,
I felt we went into the gold-medal game at the Los Angeles
Arena with some things to be concerned about.

We were playing Spain, a team I knew was very good. My
assistant on the Olympic team, Don Donoher, and I had seen

all the European national teams play, and we felt Spain, not Russia, was the best team in Europe or in the Olympic field. The Spanish coach, Antonio Diaz-Miguel, was a friend of mine who had come to Bloomington several times to watch our Indiana teams practice.

We did with him as we always did with coaches who came to see us: We opened our practices and our coaching meetings to him and gave him access to our game and practice tapes so he could know exactly how we approach things. That part didn't bother me; I knew Antonio was a good coach with a good team.

I think they proved that by winning their way into the finals, their only loss along the way a little troubling to me because it was to our team by a pretty one-sided final score, 101–68. I knew our players were aware they won that easily in a game where they hadn't even played very well in the first half.

The day of the gold-medal game, the climax to all the work we had done since the team was picked, I had Willie Davis talk to our Olympic team — the Willie Davis who was the defensive captain of the Green Bay Packers Vince Lombardi teams that won the first two Super Bowls. Bob Skoronski, those Packers teams' offensive captain, also had talked often to my Indiana teams.

This time, Willie didn't talk very long. He really said only one thing. You could see Lombardi talking instead of Willie

195

when he said, "Boys, tonight, you're going to play forty minutes of basketball that you will remember the rest of your lives, maybe even more than any other game you will ever play. Let's make damned sure it's a good memory."

That's putting something extra on it. *This game is going to stay with you forever.* Immediately, if you've got a heart and a soul, you've got to think: "He's right. This isn't going to just *happen.* We've got to *make* it happen."

The Idea Is to Win

People have asked me what was important to me as a coach. I obviously wanted a chance to coach an Olympic team and win. Even more important to me was that those twelve kids could go through life and say, "I won a gold medal in 1984." I firmly believe that would not have happened if I had just accepted them on their abilities, as great as they were.

I think — not just with the Olympic team but in every game one of my teams played — the most important thing to me was to win. To win *fairly,* to win *by the rules,* but to *win.* That helped me immeasurably to keep from losing my thoughts on the game, or the next game coming up. I did not want to put myself in a position where we had lost because of something that I didn't do or didn't see. I would look back over every game, and if I failed to do something, it upset me far more than anything the players did or didn't do.

This night, those kids on the Olympic team that Willie Davis challenged delivered just what he talked about: "Forty minutes of basketball that you will remember the rest of your lives."

Unlike our first game with Spain, this one was over at halftime. We led 52–29 and won 96–65. Every player on our team left that night with good memories, very good ones.

KNIGHT'S NUGGETS

Famous last words (coaching version):

> *Nobody in this tournament can beat Jones,*
> *so we'll save him to pitch our second game.*

> *This deep in our own territory, they'll never expect a pass.*

> *Fourth down on their two —*
> *hell with the field goal, let's go for it.*

And players' words:

> *Fast ball down the middle —*
> *that's the last thing he's expecting . . .*

> *I can hit over that water.*

> *Forget going for the tying basket — if I hit this three, we win!*

The Proud Author of a Cliché

MY WIFE, KAREN, HAD A GREAT way of telling me when I was going way too far with an issue that she considered long since settled. She could — and often did — wake me up on that with just seven words: "The horse is *dead*. Get *off* it."

That's actually an improvement on a cliché line, "Don't beat a dead horse." Don't keep an argument going that you've already won — or lost.

I know clichés are the trash heap of good writing, too trite and hackneyed even to be considered for use by — let alone having to be edited out of the copy of — all top writers. Me? I've never been counted in company like that, and I'll admit it: I'm not really an anti-cliché guy. I think some are classics.

And some, I truly believe, are at the root of this "optimism bias" — bywords ingrained into our thinking for so long that they have achieved cliché status and promised positive results that didn't and wouldn't ever come.

Then there are others I kind of like for their amusement, some for their wisdom, and at least one for which I can feel almost a parental connection — and therefore *real* fondness.

It's not hard to find a collection of phrasings that have reached cliché status. Just go to Google and tap the word *clichés*. Today's Internet offers a wide variety of shortcuts to a long, long list. I came across one collection of more than a thousand phrases that were categorized as clichés, although some of them I think would be better termed *adages* or *wise sayings*.

I heard a great story once about a sportswriter who covered a basketball game or two of ours against Illinois: Jerome Holtzman of the Chicago *Sun-Times*. Jerry was best known as a baseball writer, and he went way, way back with the Cubs and White Sox. A young sports editor named Lewis Grizzard came along at the *Sun-Times,* determined to bring sports writing at the newspaper out of the grammatical dark ages. He swore he'd absolutely, unequivocally *eliminate* clichés and jargon from *Sun-Times* sports pages, and Major League Baseball stories would henceforth include quotes from players and managers or coaches, not just writers' opinions. Times, at the *Sun-Times,* were going to damn well change!

Not long after he arrived, a Holtzman baseball story came across his desk, and the young editor made his stand. He called Jerry into his office, and in a book he wrote, Lewis Grizzard described what happened:

> I mentioned the need for quotes, and then I said, "And you use too many clichés."
>
> "Clichés?" he asked me.
>
> "Yes," I said. "You are still using worn-out baseball clichés like 'hot corner' for third base and 'circuit clout' and 'roundtripper' for home runs."
>
> Holtzman looked puzzled. Finally, he said, "Lewis, you don't understand. Those are MY clichés."
>
> I hadn't thought of that. Here was the dean of American baseball writers, and he probably did come up with those terms. And if a man invented a term, no matter how long he used it, it really couldn't be called a cliché, could it?
>
> I didn't bother with Holtzman's writing much after that.

The book was *If I Ever Get Back to Georgia I'm Gonna Nail My Feet to the Ground,* and the young sports editor was the same Lewis Grizzard who left that profession to be one of America's greatest stand-up comedians and comedy authors before dying at a terribly young age.

I loved Grizzard's comedy act, but maybe I like the

Holtzman story best because I can identify with Jerry Holtzman. In that long, long list of "clichés" I found on the Internet was the explanation I always used for why my teams never followed the latter-day trend of putting players' names on the back of their jerseys. I wanted my players always to be conscious of where their loyalty should lie:

"You're playing for the name on the front of the jersey."

Maybe somebody else said it first, I don't know. But it's in there unattributed, and I'll claim it, because *I'd* never heard anybody say it, and it's absolutely the way I thought and operated.

Besides, *everybody* should be like Jerry Holtzman and know the thrill of being the author of at least one cliché.

I maintain that clichés, if stripped of their wild-eyed optimism, can be instructive. For example:

Fools rush in where angels fear to tread.

That might be my favorite of all the wise sayings, the battle cry in the Power of Negative Thinking crusade.

Fools rush in where angels fear to tread.

Decisions. This is the time above all times not to be rushed. Don't be in a hurry. Take the time to be informed, to *know* what your best approach is. And always give yourself a one-word final question: *Why?* Why am I so sure this is right?

That advice far transcends coaching. Any person about to

make a decision needs to build in time to think carefully about it, to think: *I've heard the allure, the positives of this proposal — do I know all the potential negatives?* And always be able to say and accept an answer: *No.*

Never do today what you can put off until tomorrow — that's a tongue-in-cheek putdown of procrastination, but there's an element of the wisdom I'm preaching in that sly humor. If more people put off dumb decisions, the world would have a lot fewer of them. Better indecision than poor decision in my book.

All of that is magnified when there is money involved. *Your* money. Do I know enough to make a commitment of my money or my future? What do I really know about the guy selling this to me? You've heard that other axiom/warning:

A fool and his money are soon parted.

It's true, and you've got to be smart enough not to be the fool.

Maybe it's not even a con, just a sincere fellow with an idea that, when it works, will make him and all who believe in him rich! I'll throw in some advice that isn't a cliché but maybe should be:

Don't live someone else's dream . . . or pay for it.

Don't put a lot of money into someone else's idea. The guy is all excited . . . fine, but how many investors have dipped into their own shallow pool of savings and entered into something with a very positive thought, but have come out feeling *if only* . . .

If only I had investigated a little more . . .

If only I had stopped and thought . . .

If only I hadn't been in such a big hurry . . .

If only I had known the history of this kind of thing . . .

If only I had waited one more day . . .

If only . . .

Not just on investments, but on every decision you ever make you need to know *why*, and *why not?* A phrase that can eliminate a lot of problems in decision-making is "Let me think about it." Or "I'm not really sure about that. I need to talk to someone." Or "Let me call you back about that." Or "Give me a couple of days to study on that a little bit."

Or a slightly different tack: "Where is there any guarantee that this will work?" Or "Who do I know that's involved with this?" Or "If this is so surefire, why hasn't it been tried before?" Or, maybe best: "That sounds like a lot of bullshit to me."

All those things buy you a little time, put you in a position to think something out before making a commitment. And to do that checking. It's not a new thought. Almost exactly 500 years ago, Leonardo da Vinci said, "It is easier to resist at the beginning than at the end."

The word *no* isn't a bad way to stall when hit with a lot of sudden proposals. You can always change no into yes, and usually make people happy, but it's a lot harder—sometimes too late—to change yes to no. From our own experiences, how many times do you think people wished they could change yes into no?

Now, a leader who says no to something requested by the people he's leading should always have a good reason. It can't just be arbitrary. After time to do your own studying and evaluating, let them know: "Here's the reason we're not going to do that." And when you say yes, let them know why this is a good idea. They need to know why or why not on every decision you make on which they have an involvement.

Sometimes with my players, I simply said, "No, we're not going to do that." And maybe a little later, if I saw it was something they really wanted to do, I'd say, "I've been thinking about that. I think that would be good to do," to show them that I really did have a concern for what they wanted to do, as well as what I thought was best for them.

In all things with a yes or no option:

Stop and think.

Fools rush in where angels fear to tread.

There certainly is a coaching application. In any sport, big games can't roll around fast enough for the optimistic coach of a team that really isn't mentally ready, a team that's overconfident. An overconfident team is an indictment of its coach, not the players. Never *ever* trust your team to be ready without *your* putting those players in a position where you know damn *well* they are. And even then, I'll guarantee you that you'll sit in a locker room just before the game and wonder: *Are they really ready? Could I have done something more?* There is no sure thing.

Your job as a coach is to have your players' minds on what they have to do now — right away, in this game, to win tonight. I think that's what made me proudest of that undefeated 1975–76 Indiana team. They won so often they had every reason to think they were just better than the opponent they were about to play, but they were the best team I ever had in keeping their minds on that always paramount thing: what they had to do *now* — to win *tonight*.

A SAMPLING OF OTHER CLICHÉS I LIKE

Don't count your chickens before they're hatched.

Or victories before they're won.

Good things come to he who waits.

If he works like hell while waiting.

Haste makes waste.

But . . . don't we all?

There but for the grace of God go I.

God, and the smart basketball players He sent my way.

An ounce of prevention is worth a pound of cure.

Tell me that's not perfect Negative Thinking.

If at first you don't succeed try, try again.

And then find someone to help you.

You can't teach an old dog new tricks.

If his old tricks are good enough, don't mess with success.

Always look on the bright side.

True, if this is the "bright" that means "smart."

A bird in the hand is worth two in the bush.

My thoughts exactly when running out the clock with a lead.

Don't bite the hand that feeds you.

You might chew a little on the one that doesn't.

Don't look a gift horse in the mouth.

Translation: Make those free throws, dammit.

Get your head in the game.

Sounds like me, though I sometimes suggested extraction first.

A good beginning makes a good ending.

If accompanied by a very good middle.

All for one, one for all.

Make sure that your players feel that way.

Actions speak louder than words.

Sometimes in practice I might have been an exception.

A chain is only as strong as its weakest link.

When you have one, it's time to substitute.

Here today, gone tomorrow.

The story of too-celebrated success.

Hindsight is 20/20.

And foresight is even better.

It's not whether you win or lose, it's how you play the game.

You should be writing or broadcasting.

Take the path of least resistance.

Sounds like a Sun Tzu game plan to me.

You can lead a horse to water, but you can't make him drink.

*Maybe you haven't done enough
to make him thirsty.*

AND SOME I QUARREL WITH

Clichés and adages that preach what I consider bunk might even bear their share of responsibility for why, as the learned scientists suggest, we tend to be dangerously optimistic. For example:

You can do whatever you really believe you can do.

Now, YOU are the coach I want to play against.

You can be whatever you want to be.

Sure, jump out of a tree and try being a bird.

Hope springs eternal.

Way too often these days hope has replaced sweat.

The light at the end of the tunnel . . .

. . . is a lousy thing to rely on for vision.

The lesser of two evils . . .

. . . is still evil.

All's well that ends well.

I never was much of an "Oh, well, we won!" coach.

Boys will be boys.

Not exactly my thoughts when running a basketball team.

Damned if you do, and damned if you don't.

When that's the case, I say: Don't.

There's no use crying over spilled milk.

My theory was yelling about it a little
might prevent a recurrence.

Better the devil you know than the devil you don't know.

Better yet: Improve the company you keep.

He marches to the beat of a different drummer.

Guys like that rarely are in victory parades.

Every dark cloud has a silver lining.

The cloud is what you'd better notice.

We might be better off losing.

Is that like a doctor telling a patient,
"You might be better off dying"?

Absence makes the heart grow fonder . . .

. . . of your team without a pain in the ass who quit.

All's fair in love and war.

> *Sounds like a coach who cheats at home*
> *and on the recruiting road.*

Nice guys finish last.

> *The byword of those recruiting bad guys.*

Even a blind squirrel finds an acorn once in a while.

> *The only reason I can figure why*
> *some guys win once in a while.*

Everything's coming up roses.

> *Nice, unless you planted grapes.*

The early bird catches the worm.

> *Surely he could look around and find tastier fare.*

It will all work out for the best.

> *If you work to make it happen!*

The grass is always greener on the other side of the fence.

Be careful about what they're using over there for fertilizer.

He who lives by the sword will die by the sword.

Living without one isn't a good idea in a swordfight, either.

The blind leading the blind.

I've seen it happen, and both had whistles.

It's always darkest before the dawn.

I thought that once or twice . . . and then woke up.

What goes around comes around.

That's the way a NASCAR race always seemed to me, too.

Silence is golden.

And gets you beat if your team's on defense.

I ALSO KINDA LIKE
- -

If a frog had wings, he wouldn't bump his ass on the ground.

Another strong case for if . . . then . . .

If wishes were horses, beggars would ride.

My buddy Joe Cipriano's version: When ifs and buts are candy and nuts, what a merry Christmas it will be.

If you can't stand the heat, get out of the kitchen.

Wouldn't you like to have a Truman in the "kitchen" today?

Play the hand you're dealt.

And know when to hold 'em and when to fold 'em.

AND SOME I JUST PASS ALONG

David versus Goliath . . .

If there's a rematch, I'm betting Goliath has a slingshot, too.

The handwriting is on the wall.

When kids are given too much freedom with crayons.

Making a mountain out of a molehill.

Every sportswriter's daily challenge.

Money is the root of all evil.

But poverty isn't a whole lot better.

Banging your head against a wall.

Speaking of terrible ideas.

An acorn doesn't fall far from the tree.

I'm guessing aerodynamics is the reason.

Pull a rabbit out of a hat.

. . . but before wearing, check for residue.

Nothing ventured, nothing gained.

Bookies make a lot of money with that pitch.

Survival of the fittest.

Darwin would have made a hell of a coach.

Seeing the glass as half-empty, not half-full.

Sounds to me like pretty much the same thing.

To throw the baby out with the bathwater . . .

. . . will get you very few baby-sitting rehirings.

Slow and steady wins the race.

What was the last Olympics you watched?

The bigger they are, the harder they fall.

And quickness is the best ax to make it happen.

You can't have your cake and eat it, too.

Unless you're the biggest, meanest guy at the party.

You can't squeeze blood out of a turnip.

Or a good taste.

To the victor go the spoils.

Does the loser get the ripes?

We'll cross that bridge when we come to it.

When you think about it: Is there any other way?

What doesn't kill you makes you stronger.

Is this a definition of living on the edge?

When the going gets tough, the tough get going.

In what direction is the key.

Lightning never strikes the same place twice.

Only cheerful if the first time wasn't fatal.

Opportunity only knocks once.

Are it and lightning kin?

There, now, that wasn't so bad, was it?

Is that what's said right after the lightning strike?

Time heals all wounds.

I thought the magazine's motto was "Time wounds all heels."

It's not the size of the dog in the fight, it's the size of the fight in the dog.

But the thing to REALLY watch out for is a big fightin' dog.

POSITIVE THINKER/NEGATIVE THINKER: ADAGE

NT: Silent when unsure.

PT: Never unsure about anything.

Adage: Better to remain silent and be thought a fool than to speak out and remove all doubt. (Lincoln)

PT: No one will ever know.

NT: Wrong is wrong.

Adage: Character is what you do when no one is looking.

CONCLUSION

I'm not trying to come across as one bit smarter or wiser than you. Don't let your instincts be sugarcoated by the positive pap that has made you feel inferior and don't get swept along with can-do optimism.

Optim-ism.

Pessim-ism.

Real-ism.

The *ism* I'm arguing for is the third one: realism.

I'm not claiming to be a pioneer in this whole matter of negative teaching. You're probably a product of it yourself. Those red marks your grammar teacher put on your first English essays — they probably weren't congratulations. All of us learned what NOT to do in forming our ways to, first of all, pass Miss Thistlebottom's English class and then to learn to write, to communicate — starting with spelling, where there is always a right way and a wrong way, period.

Certainly, the "don't-do-it" emphasis is not new in sports.

Stop and think of the coaches known as "fundamental-ists"—the ones most insistent on mastering step one before even thinking about step two. It didn't start with high school coaches. One of the lines attributed to the great Greek leader Themistocles—from 500 BC, Thermopylae, and the movie *300*—was "Master yourself in simple things and then proceed to greater."

Fundamentals. Fundamentals. Fundamentals.

Fundamentals eliminate ways to fail, ways to lose. The great-est fundamentalists—in coaching, in warfare, in theology, in business—were and always have been more concerned about losing than about winning. One of the often-criticized coach-ing axioms is "playing not to lose, rather than to win." For me, playing not to lose is actually the best way to win. It's an in-grained instinct that a real winner believes to the core. Critics will say it means playing too conservatively. I understand that, but my rebuttal is if you genuinely eliminate all the ways you can lose, you're a whole lot closer to winning.

Try putting together a game-winning touchdown drive if your linemen can't go with the snap count and jump offside, if your backs haven't mastered putting the ball away to avoid fumbling when hit, if your passer doesn't check where the de-fense is as well as where his receivers are going, if the receiver doesn't look the ball into his hands rather than glance upfield to see where he can go before he has made the catch.

All of those teachings are steps toward playing not to lose, the prelude to being able to make the plays that win. There's no chicken-and-egg question here. Fundamentals come first. When you get down to the basics of any operation, the simpler the better.

There is nothing shockingly new in what I'm saying. I hope you've shared the genuine happiness, the excitement of discovery that I feel when scanning through Bartlett's *Book of Familiar Quotations,* or a similar compilation of simple thoughts that take on a profound meaning with the direct way they state convictions that we all recognize.

By the hundreds, by the thousands, I have run across someone's quoted observation about something familiar and felt, "Yeah!" or "That's so true," or "That's exactly how I feel," or sometimes even something different: "I never thought of it that way, but that's right!"

What we find in Bartlett's is the eloquence, the enduring wisdom, of great philosophers or leaders or even ordinary people with extraordinary insight. Montaigne — the great sixteenth-century French writer who invented what today we call *essays,* 200 years before Bartlett put his first list together — discussed this far better than I can.

Talking about the great thinkers who came well before him — the Chinese, the Greeks, the Romans, who analyzed our foibles and assets without the unhealthy optimism of our modern world — Montaigne described his own reactions when reading the thoughts of great writers. He would recognize a phrase that substantially had gone through his own mind before ever reading it, a thought so familiar it seemed like his own:

> If I come across by chance in the good authors, as I often do, those same subjects I have attempted to treat, seeing myself so weak and puny, so heavy and sluggish, in comparison with those men, I hold myself in pity and disdain. Still, I am pleased at this, that my opinions have the honor of often coinciding with theirs, and that at least I go the same way, though far behind them, saying, "How true!"

I hope in reading these pages a time or two you have said to yourself some version of "How true!" And maybe . . . perhaps . . . just possibly you have come away at least liberated from feeling guilty about being less than sunnily optimistic when someone is giving you a pitch.

Remember: He who hesitates may not be lost at all, except in good, healthy thought.

Negative Thinking Led Bob Knight Positively to the International Basketball Hall of Fame

INDUCTED 1991

COLLEGE BASKETBALL HALL OF FAME
Charter inductee 2006

3 NCAA CHAMPIONSHIPS
Including college basketball's last perfect season

OLYMPIC CHAMPIONSHIP 1984
Also Pan-American, NIT, Pre-Season NIT, CCA titles

902 VICTORIES
First Men's Division 1 coach to win 900

5 NATIONAL COACH OF THE YEAR AWARDS
1975, 1976, 1987, 1989, 2002

11 BIG TEN CHAMPIONSHIPS
Including the league's only two 18–0 seasons

37 STRAIGHT BIG TEN WINS
1974–1977, league record by 10

NEAR-PERFECT GRADUATION RATE
For four-year players